# CHRISTIE'S

# Rock & Pop Memorabilia

# CHRISTIE'S

# *Rock & Pop* Memorabilia

PETER DOGGETT AND SARAH HODGSON

Billboard Books
An imprint of Watson-Guptill Publications
New York

First published in New York in 2003 by Billboard Books
an imprint of Watson-Guptill Publications,
a division of VNU Business Media, Inc.,
770 Broadway, New York, NY 10003
www.watsonguptill.com

First published in Great Britain in 2003 by
PAVILION BOOKS LIMITED
Chrysalis Books
The Chrysalis Building. Bramley Road
London W10 6SP
A member of **Chrysalis** Books plc

DESIGNED BY: Sands Publishing Solutions

Library of Congress Cataloging-in Publication data for this title can be obtained
from the Library of Congress.
Library of Congress Control Number: 2002113926

ISBN 0-8230-0649-2

Set in Berkeley
Colour origination by Classicscan PTE Ltd, Singapore
Printed in Italy by Giunti Spa

1 2 3 4 5 6 7 8 9 10

*Page 2: Martin Sharp's poster design for Bob Dylan, "Mister Tambourine Man",
is one of the most desirable examples of its era.*

# contents

About Christie's    6

Introduction    8

*Chapter one*    Autographs, letters and manuscripts    32

*Chapter two*    Recordings    52

*Chapter three*    Guitars and other instruments    72

*Chapter four*    Costumes    88

*Chapter five*    Posters    104

*Chapter six*    Printed artefacts    124

*Chapter seven*    Merchandising    142

*Chapter eight*    Awards    152

*Chapter nine*    Artwork    162

Collectors' information    174

*Collectors' tips, Top ten highest priced sale items, Glossary,*
*Christie's addresses, Bibliography*

Index    187

Acknowledgements    192

# About Christie's

The name of Christie's is identified throughout the world with art, expertise and connoisseurship.

In 1766, James Christie opened his London auction house and launched the world's first fine art auctioneers. Christie's reputation was established in its early years, when James Christie's saleroom became a fashionable gathering place for Georgian society, as well as for knowledgeable collectors and dealers. Christie offered artists the use of his auction house to exhibit their works and enjoyed the friendship of leading figures of the day such as Sir Joshua Reynolds, Thomas Chippendale and Thomas Gainsborough. Christie's conducted the greatest auctions of the eighteenth and nineteenth centuries, selling works of art that now hang in the world's great museums.

Over its long history, Christie's has grown into the world's leading auction house, offering sales in over eighty separate categories, which include all areas of the fine and decorative arts, collectibles, wine, stamps, motor cars, even sunken cargo. There are hundreds of auctions throughout the year selling objects of all descriptions and catering to collectors of every level.

Buyers and browsers alike will find that Christie's galleries offer changing exhibitions to rival any museum. Unlike most museums, however, in the salerooms you can touch each object and examine it up close.

Auctions are an exciting way to buy rare and wonderful objects from around the world. In the salerooms is a treasure trove of items, and while some works may sell for prices that cause a media frenzy, many of the items offered at Christie's are affordable to even the novice collector. Insiders know that auctions are a great place to pick up exceptional pieces for sensible prices.

Rock and pop memorabilia has grown to become an important and exciting part of Christie's auction activity, since our first charity sale in 1985. From those tentative beginnings, the market has rapidly expanded in recent years, and the sale prices for the most sought-after lots have begun to rival those in more traditional auction areas, such as fine art and jewellery. Sales are staged regularly in London, New York and Los Angeles, attracting the cream of the world's specialist collectors and dealers, and raising world-record prices in many areas. Besides the normal multi-artist sales, Christie's has also held several auctions featuring unique personal collections – notably the charity sale of Eric Clapton's guitars in 1999, which offered the finest collection of rock and pop instruments ever to come under the hammer.

*Sale prices are given first in either pounds or dollars depending on whether the sale was in the UK or US. Conversions have then been calculated using an approximate exchange rate for the year of the sale and estimated figures are given in brackets.*

Nobody expected pop music to last. Until rock artists began to take themselves more seriously in the late 1960s, pop songs were supposed to be nothing more than entertainment. A new tune would appear on the radio, and listeners would either buy a copy of the record, if they could afford it, or, more likely, punch a coin into a jukebox in a bar or youth club, and dance away another three minutes of their lives. After a few

**below:** *The Beatles, who sparked a major memorabilia industry in the 1960s, remain the unrivalled market leaders.*

# INTROD

weeks, that song would vanish from the radio and the Top 30, and a new one would take its place. Few records had an active life of more than a few months.

Of course, those throwaway, ephemeral hit records of the 1950s and 1960s are now the subject of television documentaries, academic studies and a reissue industry with an annual turnover in the millions. Yesterday's forgotten 45 is now a treasured work of art, discussed by music critics with the same reverence and excitement that the art world reserves for the old masters. The leading artists from pop's golden age – the Beatles, Elvis Presley, the

Rolling Stones – have become the most famous citizens of their age. In thousands of years' time, almost every element of twentieth-century culture will have been forgotten, buried under the dust of history. But someone somewhere will still be listening to "A Hard Day's Night" and "Blue Suede Shoes".

# UCTION

Just as nobody in 1964 (even the group themselves) expected that the Beatles would still be popular ten years later, it would have been impossible to predict that memorabilia connected to pop and rock's most potent icons would one day take its place in the world's most prestigious auction rooms. But over the last two decades, pop and rock memorabilia has become one of the fastest-growing areas in the auction arena. The rarest autographs, posters, instruments and recordings from just thirty or forty years ago now regularly fetch the same kind of prices as paintings from previous centuries, or jewellery created by the doyens of the craft. This transformation of mass culture into collectible art demonstrates just how strong an impact pop and rock music has left on society since the 1960s.

*above: Handbills from the 1960s are highly sought after. This lot of three all feature the Rolling Stones.*

ONE NIGHT ONLY

**COVENTRY THEATRE** 6.0 AND 8.30

HALES STREET    Telephone 23141/2/3    COVENTRY
Administrator: JOHN SYKES    Manager and Licensee: G. K. ROBINSON

SUNDAY, 23rd MARCH

ARTHUR HOWES presents

*The Exciting Tamla-Motown Star*

**STEVIE WONDER**

"FOR ONCE IN MY LIFE"

"BUILD ME UP BUTTERCUP"

★ **THE FOUNDATIONS**

★ AMERICA'S GLAMOROUS RECORDING STARS ★

**THE FLIRTATIONS**

INTRODUCED BY

**EMPEROR ROSKO**

& FULL SUPPORTING PROGRAMME

Stalls and Circle 17/6 12/6 10/6    Upper Circle 7/6    (All seats bookable)

**above:** *Concert and tour posters, like this Stevie Wonder example from 1969, capture their era perfectly.*

It didn't happen overnight, of course. In the 1950s and 1960s, pop stars usually reckoned on a maximum of six or seven years at the top, before time and changing tastes took their inevitable toll. Elvis Presley became an international star in 1956, and by 1963 his career certainly seemed to be on the wane. That was also the year when Beatlemania hit Britain, then Europe, and then the rest of the world. But even when they were undoubtedly the most popular entertainers in the world, John Lennon, Paul McCartney, George Harrison and Ringo Starr resolutely insisted to the press that they were sure they'd be out of a job in five years' time.

Instead, their popularity never faded, even after the young girls who were their original fans moved on to the new generation of teenage idols, such as the Monkees. By 1967, when the Beatles released their *Sgt. Pepper* album, pop records were starting to be reviewed by serious music critics around the globe. Soon performers began to be divided into two camps – pop stars, who were aiming their music at the kids, and rock groups, who prided themselves on having an older and more intelligent audience, and who were attempting to deal with subjects that had previously been reserved for literature and the movies.

By the early 1970s, the rock business had exploded in influence and size. It's been growing ever since, through the heydays of prog rock and punk, new romantics and grunge, disco and funk, hip-hop and Britpop. Rock now commands a whole range of television channels, magazines and books. Almost every Hollywood film comes with a rock soundtrack, and the public pronouncements of icons

**below:** *The Jacksons signed this gatefold LP sleeve. They renamed themselves the Jackson 5 when they left their record label, Motown, in 1975.*

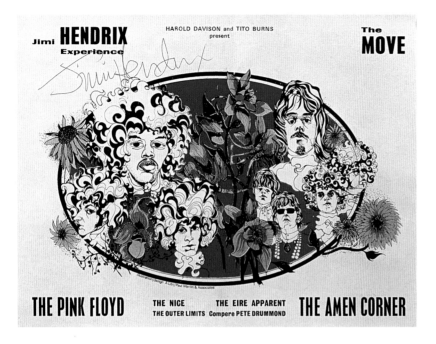

**above:** *This poster for a December 1967 concert would be a collector's item in its own right, even without Jimi Hendrix's signature.*

such as Bono from U2 and Madonna are treated more seriously by the press than the words of most politicians.

Not surprisingly, the market in pop and rock memorabilia has developed in an equally dramatic way. Back in the 1950s and 1960s, pop fans competed to get hold of their favourite stars' autographs, lining up at stage doors to win a scrawled signature from Elvis Presley, Cliff Richard or Mick Jagger. Some went as far as to tear down posters from the walls outside the clubs or concert halls where their heroes had appeared. Journalists would occasionally write stories about teenage girls who had filled their bedrooms with thousands of photos and magazine clippings about their idols. Sometimes these adoring fans even managed to attack their favourites with a pair of scissors and steal a lock of hair.

Nobody imagined at the time that any of this pop ephemera would ever have any financial value. Teenage tastes are fickle, and if a particular star went out of favour, then the photos, concert programmes and all the rest went into the bin. Occasionally, there would be a small ad in the back pages of the pop press, offering a set of Beatles autographs for sale. But there were no professional dealers, no network for buying and selling, and certainly no auctions offering exclusive items to a wider public.

It was only in the early 1970s that record collectors in Britain and America realized that they could make a little pocket money by putting together sales lists of obscure singles and albums. The first dealers specialized in records that seemed to have been forgotten by 1970 – mid-1950s rock'n'roll and rhythm & blues tracks, which had long since vanished from the record stores, and were no longer turning up on market stalls or in junkshops. Throughout the 1970s, this trend spread, and by the end of that decade there were hundreds of specialist traders operating on both sides of the Atlantic, and in many other countries as well, sending out regular auction and sales lists to their diehard clients.

At the same time, antique markets began to notice that if they offered any authentic pieces of pop memorabilia from bygone decades – posters, novelty items like Beatles wallpaper or Elvis dolls, even a gold disc or two – they were snapped up immediately. Instead of vanishing from history, as everyone had expected, the stars of the 1950s and 1960s were slowly becoming legends, like the Hollywood idols of the pre-war era. If anything, this process was happening more quickly and more dramatically. Mass-produced items from key rings to bedside lamps, which had been thrown onto the market in a hurry to cash in on Beatlemania, were now sought-after collector's items a mere decade later. People instinctively realized that there was

**below:** *This Sun single from 1955 was signed not just by Elvis but by the other members of his group, raising the price to £1,116 ($1,550) at a Christie's sale in 2001.*

a magic and an innocence about the fifteen years between the birth of rock'n'roll and the demise of the Beatles that could never be reproduced in this more sophisticated age. To this day, the vast majority of items sold at auctions around the world date from before 1970, despite the individual popularity of later artists such as Madonna and the Sex Pistols.

As the 1980s dawned, specialist collector's magazines were now being published, such as *Goldmine* in the USA, *Record Collector* in the UK and *Oldie-Markt* in Germany. Their pages were full of advertisements, not just for records, but for items of memorabilia. Yet most of the transactions carried out through those magazines were for comparatively inexpensive items.

*opposite: An array of 1960s concert programmes – easily obtainable at the time, but now collector's items.*

More valuable pieces of memorabilia were starting to come to the surface, which deserved a wider and more glittering stage.

The result was that two very different worlds – the rock industry and the refined atmosphere of the professional auction houses – came into contact, and found that they could work to each other's advantage. With their established media contacts and sturdy professionalism, the auction houses brought a new air of prestige to a trade that had previously lurked in the backstreets and market stalls. Their decades of expertise in all the different areas of the art market meant that it was no longer good enough for an item of memorabilia to be listed as a rarity; now its origins (or, as the auctioneers say, its provenance) had to be investigated and laid out for all to see. Some items were immediately exposed as fakes, but they were vastly outnumbered by the exciting new discoveries that came to light.

The kudos attached to the most famous names in the auction business brought many collectors out of the closet, who would never have bothered to wade through the small ads in

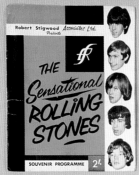

*above:* *Kiss were virtually the only rock band of the 1970s who continued the merchandising of earlier decades.*

music magazines. The regular rock memorabilia sales provided a forum for much more exclusive items to be sold than in the past. Suddenly, uniquely personal artefacts began to be offered for sale – the instruments on which some of rock's biggest stars had composed their hit records, for example, original manuscripts of song lyrics, or costumes worn on stage or in films.

With each new sale and each passing year, the market grew, and so did the prices. Every landmark auction sparked another round of press coverage, which in turn brought more choice items out into the spotlight. Some pundits reckoned that the supply of rare rock memorabilia wasn't just finite, but comparatively small, and predicted that the auction houses would soon be recycling the same material, over and over again. But they were wrong. One of the perennial miracles of the pop and rock memorabilia market is that there is always something remarkable about to be discovered – a new Beatles manuscript, perhaps, or an Elvis Presley guitar, or a set of documents signed by Jimi Hendrix, or a previously undocumented tape of the Rolling Stones before they were famous. And with each year that passes, the value of these one-off items increases, as does the legend of the stars with whom they are associated.

**below:** *The "Beatlemania" era lasted for less than three years, but the group's popularity has shown no signs of diminishing since.*

## WHO'S COLLECTIBLE

One act overshadows all their rivals in the pop and rock memorabilia market: the Beatles. More recent performers have taken advantage of the global reach of the music industry and outstripped the Beatles' record sales, but nobody has ever come close to equalling their impact.

Dozens of books have been devoted to analyzing the Beatles' success, which was based on some elusive blend of supreme songwriting talent, strong individual personalities and the emergence of a new youth culture throughout the Western world. Magic, however, is indefinable, and although it is now more than three decades since the group broke up,

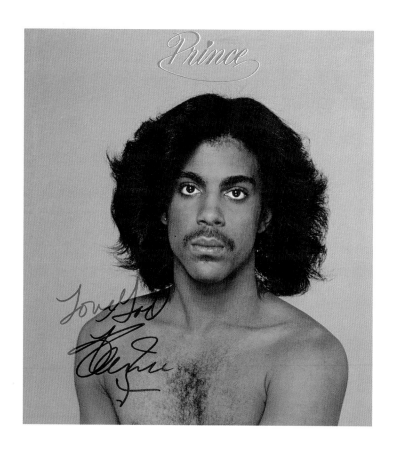

**above:** *The reclusive star Prince signed this copy of his self-titled second LP from the late 1970s with the inscription, "Love God".*

and we have sadly lost two of the four men who changed the world, successive generations of fans are still falling under the Beatles' spell.

During their remarkably brief recording career (late 1962 to early 1970), the Beatles radically transformed the way that pop music was made and brought to the public – in ways that are still being felt today. They made it possible for young stars to write and control the recording of their own material. They effectively invented the long-playing album as a vehicle for a longer and more significant statement than could be fitted onto an old vinyl single. They pioneered the art of the promotional film, which was the birth of the modern age of rock video. They were also the first pop group to form their own recording company, Apple Records, which was originally intended to be a multi-media enterprise covering almost every aspect of people's daily lives. As we will see throughout this book, all of these developments and breakthroughs have left their mark on the world of memorabilia collecting. So vast is the potential scope for collecting the Beatles that any rare or choice items even remotely connected with them – artwork by ex-member Stuart Sutcliffe, for example, personal ephemera once owned by their manager, Brian Epstein, or anything produced by their Apple Corps organization – is likely to be the subject of fierce bidding at auction.

The Beatles' closest rivals amongst other rock groups were their perennial friends and foes in the 1960s, the Rolling Stones. During their 40-year career, their image has changed from long-haired hooligans to silver-haired elder statesmen of rock-'n'roll. But as long as the central team of Mick Jagger and Keith Richards remains intact, the sound of the Stones will always have a resonance with lovers of music from that era.

Not surprisingly, it is the band's original 1960s line-up that commands most attention amongst collectors. The Stones debuted in 1963 as a six-piece, before their manager decided that keyboardist Ian Stewart didn't fit visually with the rest of the group. So he was sidelined, although he remained a loyal member of the Stones' entourage until his death in the mid-1980s. The next Stone to disappear from the story was troubled guitarist Brian Jones, who died in

**below:** *The Martin acoustic guitar used regularly at recording sessions by the Hillbilly Cat himself, Elvis Presley.*

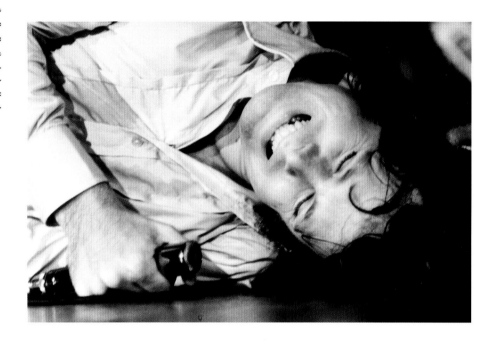

above: *Unpublished photographs, like this one by Freddie Tornberg of Doors singer Jim Morrison, attract great interest at auction.*

1969. His death marks a dividing-line in the band's history, and memorabilia from before that date is vastly more collectible than post-1970 material.

Amongst the soloists, it is only fitting that the King of Rock'n'roll, Elvis Presley, should be the most commanding figure. He began recording in 1954 for the tiny independent label, Sun Records – which was also the starting point for the careers of such major US stars as Johnny Cash, Roy Orbison, Jerry Lee Lewis, Carl Perkins and Charlie Rich. But it was only when he moved to the major label RCA Records at the start of 1956 that he took off in commercial terms. Within six months he was the biggest star in America, and by the end of that year, a succession of hit records – and his first movie, *Love Me Tender* – had brought the so-called "Hillbilly Cat" to the rest of the world.

Presley's career sagged in the 1960s under the weight of too many sub-standard film roles, but he made a comeback at the end of that decade. For several years, his live shows in Las Vegas and on tour won ecstatic reviews, but gradually he began to lose control of his life and his health. By the time he died, overweight and prematurely old at the age of just forty-two, he was regarded as a sad, rather ridiculous figure by much of the media. His fans remained loyal, however, and gradually the rest of the world began to appreciate what they had lost.

Each passing year adds another layer of mystique to the Elvis legend, and the market in Presley memorabilia has boomed as a result.

That same strange process of life after death has affected many other rock casualties. For almost a decade after his squalid demise in 1971, Jim Morrison, the lead singer of the Doors, was a forgotten figure. It took a sensational best-selling biography, followed by a Hollywood film, to transform this 1960s poet, songwriter and self-styled "shaman" from a has-been into an icon around the world. As with Elvis, his reputation keeps on growing, as does the demand for anything he touched or wrote, including stage costumes, manuscripts, letters and gold records.

It's hard to believe it now, but there was a time in the mid-1970s when Jimi Hendrix was also in danger of being forgotten. He died in still mysterious circumstances in 1970, less than four years after the release of his debut single, "Hey Joe". He enjoyed two years of enormous commercial success and musical fulfilment, and then two more of business complications, personal crises and artistic self-doubt. Yet what was undeniable throughout it all was that Hendrix was the most

**above:** *A contact sheet of unpublished photographs of Jimi Hendrix on stage at the Star-Club in Hamburg, Germany, in 1967.*

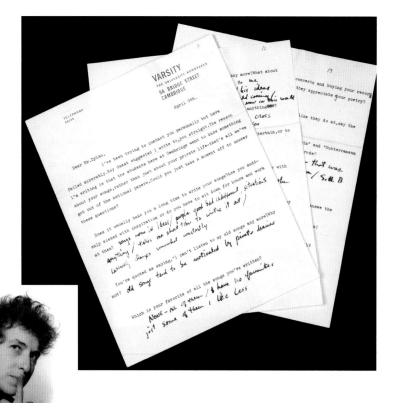

influential and explosive musician of the rock era. During the 1980s, the rock world finally began to come to terms with his legacy, and his supreme vision as an artist – plus his undoubted visual appeal – has helped to maintain a keen market for his memorabilia.

Sadly, there is nothing like premature death to stoke the fires of a legend. It's been called "James Dean syndrome" – the realization that by dying young, with so much potential unfulfilled, a performer will always retain his or her charisma. We will never see them getting old; the enigma of what they might have achieved if they had lived will never be answered.

Besides the obvious cases we've already mentioned, the "James Dean syndrome" has created a market for items connected with many other rock'n'roll casualties – 1950s stars Buddy Holly and Eddie Cochran; reggae genius Bob Marley; punk rocker Sid Vicious; acid-rock legend Janis Joplin; soul star Marvin Gaye; grunge icon Kurt Cobain. In every case, the finite limit to their careers and their lives has boosted the demand for artefacts connected with them, the more personal and poignant the better.

*above:* *A questionnaire from a student newspaper filled in (but never returned) by Bob Dylan during his 1965 UK tour.*

The memorabilia market isn't solely restricted to a morbid interest in lost icons, though. Many artists whose careers are still flourishing attract enormous interest when unique items are offered at auction. They tend to be either charismatic figures whose mystique remains intact, musical pioneers, or ideally both. Bob Dylan is perhaps the archetypal figure in the last category. Still actively touring and recording in his sixties, he seems to have lost none of the sense of mystery that attracted a generation of diehard followers in the mid-1960s. With someone like Dylan, less exclusive items of memorabilia, such as autographs, don't fetch huge prices, simply because he is still available today to sign some more. What fetch the really big sums in his case are things like early drafts of his lyrics, personal letters, and acetate versions of songs that he never released to the public. He is a prime example of a performer whose creativity counts for more than his celebrity at auction.

Madonna is undoubtedly the most collectible new artist of the last two decades. Her appeal is very different to Dylan's, being based as much on her visual image and style as the content of her records. As a result, Madonna collectors are particularly

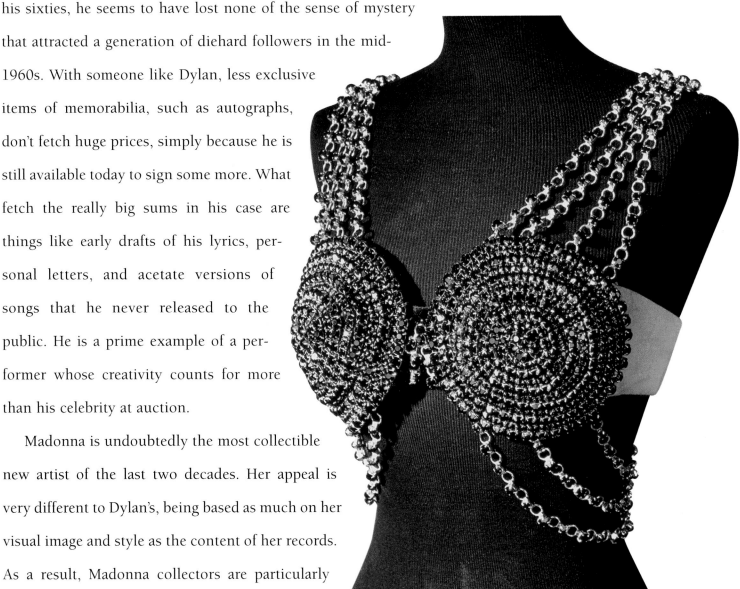

**below:** *This bustier, an example of Madonna's unmistakeable stage gear, was worn by her on the 1987 "Who's That Girl" tour.*

**right:** *This set of Rolling Stones autographs from 1963 was sent to the secretary of their Official Fan Club.*

National Secretary:-

**Miss Diane Nelson**

**86 Furze Lane**

**Farncombe**

**Nr. Godalming**

**Surrey**

drawn to her dramatic stage costumes and jewellery – the more exotic, the better.

Apart from Madonna, there are major pop stars from recent decades who have a solid fan base and often attract interest at auction. Into this category come artists like David Bowie, Queen, Eric Clapton and Prince – who have some of the most loyal and enthusiastic fans in the history of pop. As yet, however, that support hasn't translated fully into the auction market, with the result that Madonna items would usually outsell them all.

In the late 1990s, there was a surge of interest at auction in contemporary stars, such as the Spice Girls, Britney Spears and Oasis. It is still too early to predict whether this will translate into a lasting impact on the memorabilia market, or whether prices will decline once their status in the pop charts ebbs away.

It's important at this stage to highlight the difference between prestigious memorabilia auctions and the day-to-day trade in rare records and ephemera. Both *Record Collector* (in Britain) and *Goldmine* (in America) have published extremely weighty price guides to collectible records, CDs and cassettes, listing tens of thousands of different performers, many of them obscure even to experts in the field.

As we'll see in Chapter Two, the record collecting market exists in its own right, covering a much wider range of areas and artists than will ever be represented at a top auction. It's a market for specialists, as there are often only a few collectors around the world competing for the most precious rock'n'roll, punk or soul rarities. With very few exceptions, these records don't do well in the major rock auctions; instead, they usually sell via the network of dealers and collectors.

There are also many stars from every era of popular music who command a faithful fan club, often numbering thousands of people, but who make little impact on the pop and rock memorabilia markets. As with rare records, this is a case where supply and demand really comes into play. Fan club members will often pay each other huge prices for rare records or pieces of memorabilia that, in the wider market, don't have any great value. With all areas of collecting, an item is only worth what someone is prepared to pay for it. It is often the case that something that might fetch a sizeable sum in the hothouse arena of a fan club convention might only raise a small fraction of that amount at a memorabilia auction in London or New York. The top auction houses aren't guided solely by price when it comes to choosing what items to put in a sale.

Quality plays an equally important role. A superb piece of Beatles or Elvis Presley memorabilia will always attract more attention and interest from the public and the media than an incredibly obscure, privately pressed album by a bunch of unknown musicians – even if the eventual selling prices are more or less the same. Auction houses always want to boost public awareness of their specialist areas, and luminaries such as the Beatles have infinitely more pulling-power and prestige than performers who weren't even famous in their own home towns.

*below: Buddy Holly's tragic death in 1959 ensured that anything bearing his autograph became an instant collector's item.*

THE CRICKETS *Exclusive Coral Recording Artists*

COPYRIGHT

## WHAT'S COLLECTIBLE

The same highly selective judgement has to go into deciding what kinds of memorabilia are likely to become collector's items, and which of these qualify for inclusion in a sale at a top auction house. Once again, there is a wide gulf between items that are considered collectible and those that attract high prices.

Many collectors are "completists" – in other words, they want to obtain every possible kind of artefact connected with their chosen artist or era. The term particularly applies to record collectors, who often choose to track down every release by a certain performer, to the extent that they end up with multiple copies of the same record because they have minor variations in their packaging or contents. The intrinsic value of many of these items may be very small – only a few pounds or dollars in many cases – but they can prove to be just as elusive as some much more expensive items. However, you wouldn't expect to find such low-priced records on sale in the auction room.

Auction houses concentrate almost entirely on items that are exclusive, and

**below:** *A Pocket Pal Hohner harmonica, which was signed by Bob Dylan and used by him on several occasions in the 1980s and 1990s.*

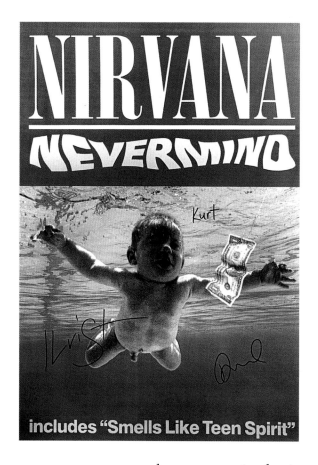

*above:* Kurt Cobain's tragic death in 1994
created immediate demand for items such as
this signed Nirvana poster.

preferably unique. Artefacts with a personal connection to a star performer are particularly sought after. They might have been owned by a top artist, worn or played on stage at a significant event, or simply autographed by a star. Whatever the exact circumstances, that personal touch can give them an add-on value far exceeding the intrinsic worth of the artefact itself. As an example, a concert programme from a Beatles tour in 1963 may be worth a modest amount, perhaps £50 to £70 ($75–$100). But if it has been signed by the group, then that price would automatically rise to several thousand pounds.

There are exceptions to this rule, of course. In some cases, memorabilia that doesn't have that personal link to the performer is equally valued by collectors. In the case of records, for example, there are certain classic rarities that have achieved a stellar status of their own in the collecting world, such as the Beatles' "butcher cover" (see Chapter Two). Limited edition prints, posters and books are also keenly collected – though, as usual, the most significant factor here is the connection with a major artist. A 1950s concert poster featuring a star such as Elvis Presley may actually be easier to find than a similar item featuring a much more obscure artist, such as Elvis's Sun Records stablemate, Sonny Burgess. But unless the potential purchaser specialized in collecting Sun ephemera, you would almost always expect the Elvis item to fetch the higher price.

**left:** *A souvenir poster from the late 1960s of Jimi Hendrix, whose tragically early death in 1970 established him as an enduring rock icon.*

Perhaps the strangest kinds of collectible pop and rock items are those that were mass-produced, perhaps in runs of several hundred thousand or even a million, but that were regarded as throwaway items at the time, and hence haven't survived in any quantity. In 1964, America was swamped with Beatles merchandising, as manufacturers looked for a quick and easy dollar by producing every imaginable kind of item, from curtains to Beatle wigs, bearing the Beatles' name, likenesses or facsimile signatures. Teenage fans bought these items in enormous quantities, but almost all of this memorabilia ended up being discarded, damaged or destroyed. Only a tiny proportion has survived complete with its original packaging, and these items can now sell for prices hundreds of times higher than their original retail value.

One major factor that plays a key role in establishing the value of any potential collector's item is its provenance – the story of how it came to exist, where it came from, and how it reached its current owner. Many items authenticate themselves, such as records, posters and concert programmes. Others require experts from auction houses to test their credentials, by comparing them with other examples of a star's handwriting, for example, or checking the serial numbers of a potentially rare guitar. But there are many items where outside evidence of how the artefact was obtained is almost as important as the item itself. As we will see in the next chapter, there is no area of memorabilia collecting for which this is more vital than autographs, manuscripts and other signed items.

**left:** *The Doors, with lead singer Jim Morrison second from the left. His signature sold for £646 ($910) at a sale in 2001.*

*chapter one*

The desire to collect personal keepsakes of famous people has existed as long as celebrity itself. Long before the twentieth-century invention of mass culture and global stardom, admirers of leading military and political figures, and notorious writers such as Lord Byron and Oscar Wilde, vied to obtain any item linked to their heroes – a lock of Byron's hair, perhaps, a manuscript of Wilde's, or something as ordinary as a comb that was given unexpected lustre by having been used by Admiral Nelson aboard HMS *Victory*.

The most familiar artefact of this kind is the autograph. There is evidence that signatures of the famous and infamous were being collected as early as the eighteenth century. Certainly from the start of the twentieth century onwards, adoring fans regularly congregated outside stage doors in the hope of obtaining the signature of a leading man or lady. The invention of the feature film introduced audiences around the world to actors whom they could never expect to meet, but who felt like personal friends, thanks to the imaginary intimacy provided by the cinema screen. Radio, records and television accelerated this process, and the autograph hunter rapidly became a standard ingredient of a life in showbiz.

Why do people collect signatures? An autograph can act as proof that you have met a celebrity, particularly if he or she has added a specific dedication or message to their standard signature. Graphologists set great store by handwriting as a key to personality, and some collectors no doubt imagine that they can gain insight into their hero's character from a few words scrawled on a photograph or sheet of paper.

Ultimately, our signature is our method of demonstrating our identity in the modern world, where we can be required to sign our names in order to obtain money from a bank, use a credit card, or check in at a gym or club. Every time we sign, we are leaving our unique

**below:** *The most valuable sets of Rolling Stones signatures are those that include guitarist Brian Jones's, who died in 1969.*

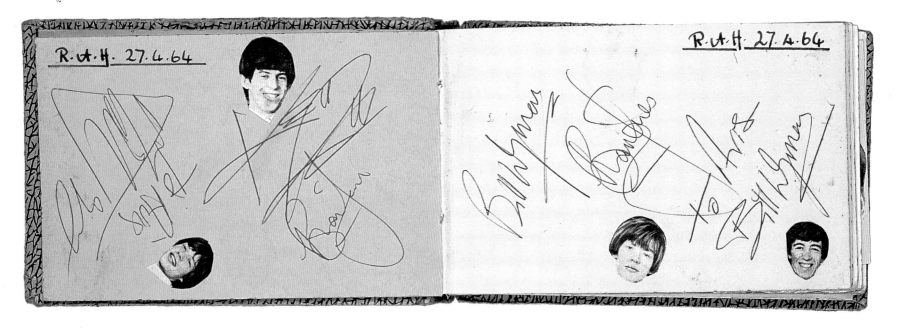

personal mark on a document or register – so it is easy to see why a fan of a film star or recording artist takes particular pride in obtaining an example of their signature.

In theory, nothing should be easier to authenticate than a signature. You go backstage at a concert hall, meet your idol, ask them to sign their name in an autograph book or programme, and come away with a priceless souvenir – and, quite possibly, a valuable collector's item of the future. If you're very fortunate, then a friend or relative will be there to document the meeting for posterity via a photograph or videotape, providing incontrovertible proof that you and the star were both present when the item was signed.

Such meetings are comparatively rare, however. A large proportion of autographs are obtained in less personal circumstances. You might write to the artist's management or record company and receive a signed photo by return, for example. Or you might leave your autograph book with a minder or roadie, and return later to pick up the prized message and signature. Under either of these circum-

**above:** *This set of autographs by the Jimi Hendrix Experience went under the hammer for £1,057 ($1,480) in a 2001 sale.*

In the case of the Beatles, the volume of mail they received at the zenith of Beatlemania was so large that their fan club couldn't cope. A minor scandal was narrowly averted after a newspaper discovered that thousands of letters from fans were being dumped without ever being opened. As a result, anyone who spent any time around the Beatles' entourage – not just their own staff but visiting journalists and photographers – was regularly asked to help out by signing their share of photos for fans. The group's two road managers, Neil Aspinall and Mal Evans, became adept at signing on behalf of the boys when the need arose, which was almost constantly when they were on the road; so much so that these two "secretarial signatures" have become instantly recognizable to the trained eye.

stances, what seems like a souvenir of a star might turn out to be something less desirable.

It has become common knowledge in recent decades that many top stars employ office staff to fake their autographs – and produce what have become known as "secretarial signatures". The motives are usually perfectly valid: a pop band at the height of their celebrity might receive tens of thousands of letters a month, and even the sternest critic of the pop business wouldn't expect the stars to answer them all personally. With a little practice, the stars' assistants, telephonists and friends can easily learn to reproduce their autographs so effectively that it is extremely difficult for the untrained eye to tell the difference between the fakes and the real thing.

**above:** *An RCA Victor souvenir calendar card for 1966, and a King of Hearts playing card – both signed by Elvis Presley.*

Another person who learned the trick of signing for all four Beatles was George Harrison himself, who used to amuse himself in his post-Beatles days by reeling off all four signatures when he was asked for his own autograph. Like the rest of the secretarial signatures, George's "forgeries" looked almost exactly like the originals.

"Forgeries" of another kind can also be a problem. Sets of Beatles signatures appeared on many pieces of merchandising and memorabilia in the mid-1960s, and it was simple for devious people to copy or trace them onto a sheet of paper, and then announce that they had some valuable Beatles autographs for sale.

Fortunately, there are subtleties and nuances obvious only to the expert that allow auction houses to differentiate the vast majority of fakes and secretarial signatures from the real thing. The task becomes much easier if there is an additional message besides the signature. It's one thing to copy John Lennon's autograph from a 1960s magazine; it's quite another to fabricate a specimen of Lennon's handwriting even for a simple message such as "With lots of love from . . .". As a result, collectors always prefer signatures with an extra message; in the case of the Beatles, it's sufficient for just one of the group to have scrawled a few extra words. In their initial months of fame, for instance, one of the Beatles would usually add the group's name in brackets after their signature – presumably to help the fan remember who these obscure pop singers were!

When it comes to buying autographs, purchasers attending a sale at an auction house are protected by a Limited Warranty for a period of five years from the date of the sale. In the unlikely event that a signature was sold and later proved to be a forgery, the buyer would be entitled to a full refund. But what can you do if you are buying from a private collector or a dealer?

This is where provenance becomes very important. As we've already mentioned, the ideal proof is a visual record of the meeting where the autograph was obtained. Failing that, then the seller should be able to provide details of where and when the artists signed their names. Maybe they'll have a concert programme that will go a long way towards proving that they were actually there on the day in question. Or they will be able to show that they lived in a particular area when the star was on location or on vacation there. Background knowledge about the artist is always useful: Elvis Presley collectors, for instance, would probably know that "the King" didn't play any live

concerts between 1961 and 1968, and would therefore turn down any signature supposedly obtained at such an imaginary event. But the same kind of knowledge can help to authenticate an item that, on the surface, seems far more dubious. Could Presley really, for example, have signed his name at the Folies Bergère, the exotic niterie in Paris, in the late 1950s? It seems unlikely – but the reference books show

**above:** *A rare signed publicity photo of the High Numbers from 1964. A few months later they changed their name to the Who.*

that during his time in the US Army in Germany, he was allowed to visit the French capital for a weekend furlough, and did indeed sign a programme from the risqué cabaret club for a fan.

Careful checking of the signature and the paper on which it sits is also very important. You'd automatically be suspicious if someone claimed to have an Elvis signature from the mid-1950s that had been done with a felt-tip pen, for example. Likewise, some amateur forgers have attempted to sell John Lennon or Jimi Hendrix signatures on record sleeves that were

only issued after their deaths. They may have been musical geniuses, but even Lennon and Hendrix couldn't have signed autographs from beyond the grave.

As with so much other memorabilia, the grave sadly plays its part when it comes to autographs. Once a performer or group member has died, the value of their signature automatically rises, for the logical reason that they won't be around to provide any more. Sets of Rolling Stones autographs from the 1960s, which include Brian Jones's name, are worth much more than those from a few years later, after first Mick Taylor and then Ronnie Wood replaced the late guitarist. By contrast, the original line-up

**below:** *The recording contract signed by the Sex Pistols during a notorious ceremony outside Buckingham Palace in London.*

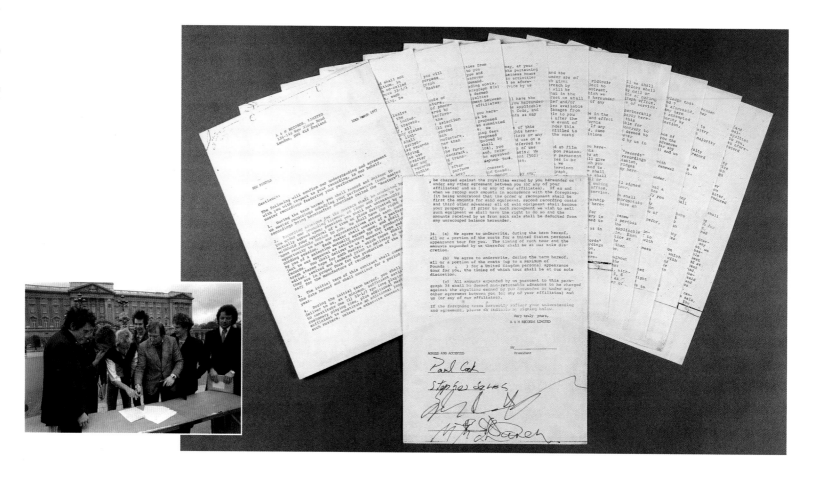

of the Sex Pistols, featuring Glen Matlock on bass, produced less valuable signatures than the second incarnation of the band, which included the late Sid Vicious.

Many pop signatures come onto the market in period autograph books, in which a fan gradually assembled a collection from a variety of pop, TV and film stars. These tend to be worth much less than the individual values of all the signatures they contain, so for a relatively small outlay you can often obtain a book that will include the autographs of many of the leading performers of the 1950s and 1960s.

## CONTRACTS

Although it might not have the nostalgic appeal of a signature obtained when you met a favourite star, a legal document or contract bearing an autograph is a very choice piece of memorabilia indeed. One particularly fine example was sold at Christie's in London in 2000. It was the recording contract with A&M Records that was signed by the members of the Sex Pistols in March 1977, during a well-publicized and provocative ceremony outside Buckingham Palace at the height of the Queen's Silver Jubilee celebrations. Not only does the document include the handwriting of all four Pistols, including the late Sid Vicious, plus their manager Malcolm McLaren, but it dates from one of the most notorious events in their entire career. Although the paper itself is only a mimeographed copy (the legal signing of the agreement had already taken place in private), the fact that the signatures were authentic and that the ceremony was such a high-profile occasion sent the price soaring to £3,525 (over $5,000).

When the Beatles signed a regular weekly docket in spring 1961, allowing their employers at the Top Ten Club in Hamburg, Germany, to release their wages, they could never have imagined that the documents would have any significance. Yet in a series of sales in 2001 and 2002 Christie's was able to sell ten of the thirteen dockets which had been handwritten and signed some forty years earlier, before the Beatles' rise to fame. They were not only fascinating artefacts in themselves, dating from a relatively obscure time in the group's history, but they also offered an opportunity for collectors to purchase vintage signatures by the original line-up that featured Pete Best on drums, rather than Ringo Starr. The documents also included the handwriting of the group's occasional collaborator in Hamburg, British rock'n'roller Tony Sheridan. His signature isn't worth a great deal by itself, but his contribution to these contracts undoubtedly gave them an extra degree of interest to the knowledgeable collector – and boosted the top price to more than £18,000, over $25,000.

## LETTERS

Like autographs, personal letters have long been treasured for the intimate insight they provide into the lives of the talented and famous. No set of collected works by a major author is complete without an anthology of their correspondence – though the modern preference for conducting both pleasure and business by telephone and e-mail seems set to make this custom a thing of the past.

Fortunately, the letter was still the most common form of long-distance communication in the 1950s and 1960s, when the kings of the rock and pop memorabilia world were in their prime. Not that the likes of Elvis Presley or the Beatles had much opportunity to correspond with the tens of thousands of fans who wrote to them. Members of the Beatles and the Rolling Stones used to send personal replies to fan letters at the dawn of their careers, when it was still a novelty for them to be the centre of so much attention. A charming episode of the cartoon series *The Simpsons* portrayed the animated Ringo Starr still working through his 1960s fan letters in the early 1990s, and sending Marge Simpson an overdue response to the portrait she had sent him nearly thirty years earlier. But that was on television: a real life Marge Simpson would have been extremely unlikely to have received any response from Ringo or the other Beatles, unless she was writing from Liverpool in 1962 and was an old acquaintance of the band.

As a result, there's a particularly magical innocence to the few surviving examples of pop stars writing personally to their fans. John Lennon, Paul McCartney and George Harrison all sent letters home to fans while they were playing at the Star-Club in Hamburg, and several years later, both Lennon and Harrison replied to letters they'd received while they were studying meditation in India with the Maharishi Mahesh Yogi. Both Beatles had been asked for money by Indian fans; as John Lennon told his correspondent, "If every request like yours was granted there would be no 'huge treasure' as you call it. . . All you need is initiative – if you don't have this I suggest you try transcendental meditation through which all things are possible." Within a few weeks, of course, Lennon had lost much of his faith in both the Maharishi and meditation – while the lucky recipient of his letter ended up with something that was worth much more than the cash handout he had originally requested!

A letter of now historic interest was received by Bobby Brown, the secretary of the first Beatles Fan Club, in 1962. Her correspondent was Paul McCartney, then ensconced with the rest of the Beatles at the Star-Club in

**opposite:** *These remarkable questionnaires were filled out by the Rolling Stones in 1963 and sent to the secretary of their fan club.*

Hamburg, Germany. He was full of enthusiasm for the group's forthcoming recording sessions in the city: "We'll probably make one or two backing (Tony) Sheridan as well as the ones on our own, and Brian (Epstein)'s going to see about having them released in England as soon as possible." The session took place, but Epstein's plans were interrupted when the Beatles were offered an audition with George Martin at Parlophone Records.

In her guise as the Rolling Stones' fan club secretary, Doreen Pettifer received several remarkable documents – including biographical lifelines, filled in by each of the original band members (all, at least, except pianist Ian Stewart, who was exiled from the group just before their first single was released, on the grounds that he didn't fit in visually with the rest). These information sheets, filled in with off-the-cuff humour by the Stones, later appeared both as fan club and press handouts. In particular, Keith Richards used the occasion to insert some private jokes, referring to the colour of his eyes as "Brown (& bloodshot)", and adding the words "nanker-nankering" to an otherwise conventional list of personal likes. A few months later, the nonsense word "nanker" passed into pop legend, when Jagger and Richards credited their early self-composed songs to the mythical "Nanker & Phelge".

Given the Rolling Stones' carefully manufactured anti-establishment image, it was amusing to see another letter from the group – typed but signed by all five members – that emerged at auction in 2000. It was written to the local head of police in Bournemouth in Southern England, thanking them for "all the kind help given by yourself and the men under your command" during the group's recent concert there in 1964. Within a few months, the Stones had suffered the first of a long series

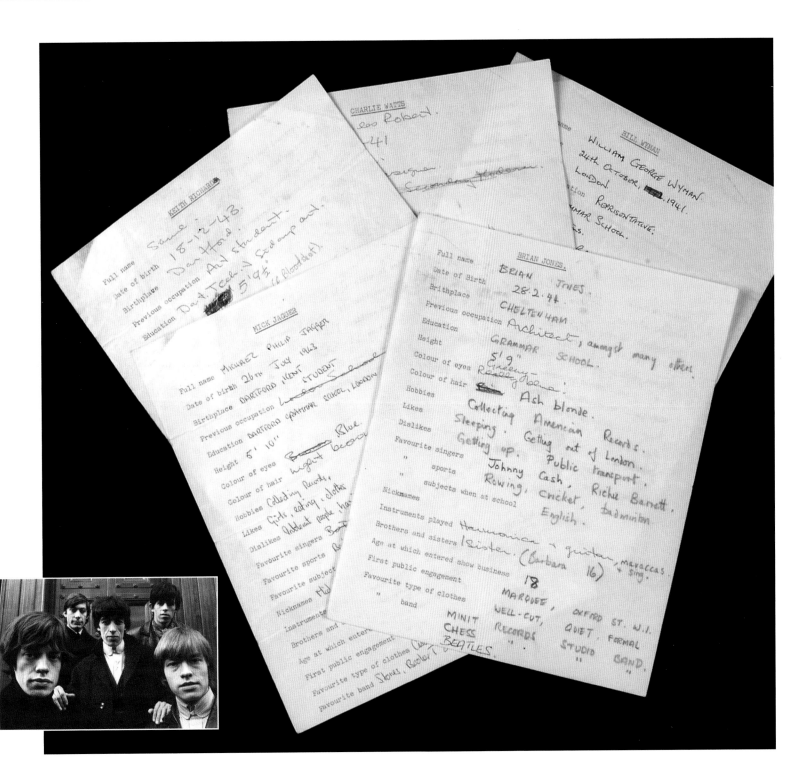

of arrests and run-ins with the law, so this was probably the last such letter of its kind.

Not all rock star correspondence that has surfaced at auction has been quite so good-humoured. Between 1969 and 1971, as relations between the group members soured and nearly broke down completely, John Lennon and Paul McCartney sent a series of inflammatory letters back and forth – sometimes to each other, but more often using the British pop press as a platform for a very public debate.

In recent years, Christie's has sold several original manuscripts or typescripts of this kind, usually sent by Lennon to the pop weekly *Melody Maker*, and each one provoking an equally fiery response in print from McCartney a week or two later.

Yet the most outspoken letter of this kind, which came up for auction in spring 2001, was meant for McCartney's eyes only. The so-called "rant" letter exists only in handwritten draft form, and there is no confirmation that it was actually sent by Lennon to his former best friend and songwriting partner. Obviously inspired by a similar missive from the McCartneys, it opened unpromisingly – "I was reading your letter and wondering what middle-aged cranky Beatle fan wrote it" – and went downhill from there.

Lennon attacked Linda McCartney ("Linda – if you don't care what I say – shut up! Let Paul write") and her family ("all this petty shit that came from your insane family") and seemed to suggest that he believed the McCartney marriage would soon be over ("God help you Paul – see you in two years – I reckon you'll be out then"). Further enraging Paul, no doubt, he lashed out again at

**opposite:** *The revealing (if not always honest) letter sent by Elvis Presley to his girlfriend, actress Anita Wood, c. 1959.*

Linda and "your petty little perversion of a mind, Mrs McCartney". Even amongst long-time colleagues who had always been outspoken with each other, this was powerful (not to say insulting) stuff, written in the white heat of the moment, and obviously never intended to be read by the general public. Yet thirty years on, it testifies to the extreme strain that the Beatles' business problems put upon their personal relationships. Yesterday's anguish and argument have become today's history lesson – and also a prime slice of rock memorabilia, which eventually sold for some £60,000 ($84,000).

Equally personal was the letter that Paul McCartney sent to the Beatles' troubled manager, Brian Epstein, presumably at the time of one of Epstein's nervous breakdowns or suicide attempts. It was one of the items that Epstein passed on to his chauffeur Brian Barrett for safekeeping shortly before his death in 1967, and that came up for auction more than thirty years later, after all of Epstein's closest family members had also passed on.

The letter revealed both McCartney's extreme affection for Epstein, and also the Beatles' collective impatience with his increasingly disorganized and dangerous lifestyle. "You are ill again," he wrote. "If I am right in thinking your 'sick periods' are caused by events rather than germs, then I would like to echo the vicar. Your BIGGEST TROUBLE IS THAT YOU TAKE IT ALL TOO SERIOUSLY."

Nothing could be further removed from the serious tone of these letters than the love letter sent by Elvis Presley from his army location in Germany, to his then girlfriend at home, actress Anita Wood. Since Presley's death, of course, we have learned plenty about his sexual exploits and romantic adventures during his time in Germany between 1958 and 1960, but when Anita Wood received this endearingly naïve letter, she must have felt entirely certain of her famous boyfriend's affections.

"Dear 'Little Bitty'," the missive began. "You'll never know how much I miss you baby, and how much I want to pet you and call you 'Widdle Bitty' . . . I guarantee that when I marry it will be Miss 'Little Presley' Wood . . . Just remember this is a guy that loves you with all his heart and wants to marry you." Ironically, in view of what we now know about Presley's own extra-curricular activities, he insisted that the only barrier to their union was infidelity:

**right:** *A simple letter from one Savoy Hotel guest to another, penned by Joan Baez to Bob Dylan in 1965.*

**below:** *A piece of rock history from 1965: a rare postcard from Donovan to his idol, Bob Dylan.*

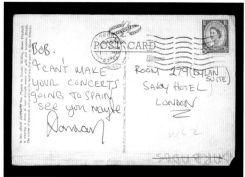

rant or the Elvis billet-doux. Several business letters have been sold at auction, as have brief thank-you notes, or requests for information, which reveal little of the character or importance of the sender. But as long as they are signed, they remain of great value to specialist collectors.

It's not surprising that the more personal the correspondence, the higher the price it is likely to fetch at auction. One unusual collection of paper ephemera, which was auctioned at Christie's in spring 2002, centred around Bob Dylan – and once again had taken more than three decades to reach the saleroom. The collection, which sold for £8,225 ($12,300), dated from Dylan's 1965 British tour. This tour marked the dividing-line between his original incarnation as an acoustic folk singer of mostly protest material, and the electric folk-rocker who was about to transform the nature of the popular song forever. Unusually, apart from a simple autograph on a blank piece of paper, only one item in the lot was written in Dylan's hand – a questionnaire about his songwriting methods and philosophy, which had been sent to the singer by the Cambridge University students' magazine, *Varsity*. At that time, Dylan was treating most interviewers with barely concealed contempt, but he felt kindly enough disposed towards the Cambridge students to fill out the questionnaire quickly but with some care. Sadly, at that point his spirit of co-operation ran out, and he never returned the questionnaire to its sender in the stamped addressed envelope provided.

Included in the same Christie's lot was a small bunch of correspondence addressed to Dylan that shed some light on his turbulent personal life at the time of the UK tour. There was a postcard from his supposed British rival, Donovan, who had apparently decided to avoid another meeting-cum-confrontation with his American idol. The

"Love me, trust me and keep yourself clean and wholesome," he begged his girlfriend, "because that is one big thing that can determine our lives and happiness together."

Sadly, of course, the marriage between "the King" and his "Little Widdle Bitty" never took place. Instead, Elvis was eventually wed to a young girl who had been much closer to hand during the German years, army sergeant's daughter Priscilla Beaulieu. Their correspondence, if it exists, has sadly never come up for auction. The letter to Anita Wood, meanwhile, sold for almost £20,000, or nearly $30,000, in 2001.

Not all surviving correspondence from the rock greats is quite as personal – or as candid – as the Lennon

exotic actress and future Velvet Underground singer Nico sent Dylan a note to remind him that he had promised to write her some songs. Most poignantly, there was a loving get-well message from his some-time girlfriend Joan Baez, who had arrived in Britain during a brief vacation in Europe to discover that Dylan was confined to his hotel room with a serious illness. Her note was more straight-forward than Dylan's romantic life, as unknown to Baez at that time, he was holed up at the Savoy Hotel in London with the woman who was about to become his wife. What appeared on the surface to be a simple and short letter from a friend turned out in context to be an unsuspecting farewell to a former lover.

Even if the background to these choice items of correspondence isn't always clear to the outside eye, you wouldn't need to be an expert in the auction field to be able to tell that letters in the hand of artists as prominent as John Lennon, Paul McCartney, Brian Jones, Elvis Presley or Bob Dylan would be likely to be valuable collector's items today.

Yet not every item bearing one of those legendary names is what it seems to be – for example "secretarial signatures", written on the star's behalf by his or her staff (see page 36). Not surprisingly, there is also plenty of secretarial correspondence about – not just letters signed "pp" ("per pro" in Latin, or "on behalf of") for the star, the way that a PA would sign for a businessperson who was out of the office, but items that appear on the surface to have been written by the performer himself.

This most often applies in the case of Elvis Presley. His manager, Colonel Tom Parker, regularly sent letters, birthday cards, telegrams and the like to business associates and friends from "Elvis and the Colonel". The unsuspecting recipient might have assumed at the time that these items had been signed by Presley himself. But comparison of handwriting proves that the signature was usually provided by the Colonel, or even one of his office staff. On some occasions, of course, letters were probably signed by Elvis on the part of himself and the Colonel, but it's fair to say that many people who considered themselves to be great personal buddies of Elvis probably had Christmas cards from him on proud display, not realizing that Presley not only hadn't signed them, but probably didn't even know they'd been sent. But that's show business.

## LYRICS

The handwritten items discussed in this chapter have gradually taken us closer and closer to the heart of rock's most iconic performers – from simple autographs, to business contracts, to personal letters. In the case of song-writers, however, nothing is more central to their art than their song lyrics; and manuscripts of some of rock's most famous songs, scrawled by the hand that originally wrote them, represent some of the most desirable and valuable items of rock memorabilia ever sold at auction.

As the rock auction market has revealed, great song-writers have very different attitudes to the pieces of paper on which they write out the first drafts of their work. Many of them obviously regard these sets of lyrics as the ultimate pieces of their own memorabilia, and guard them with great care. When George Harrison prepared his limited edition autobiography, *I Me Mine*, at the end of the 1970s, he was able to call on an incredible archive of his own lyrics. He'd written them on hotel notepaper, airport postcards, in-flight notelets and every imaginable kind of scrap paper; but each one had been lovingly filed away for the day when they could be exhibited to the world via a deluxe limited edition book. (The original *I Me Mine* is a collector's item in its own right, in fact, as we'll see in Chapter Six.)

Yet Harrison's colleagues in the Beatles weren't always so careful. Several examples of lyrics in the handwriting of John Lennon or Paul McCartney have surfaced at auction in recent times, and they have all sold for phenomenal sums of money.

In 2000, Christie's Los Angeles saleroom auctioned a unique set of lyrics for John Lennon's 1970 solo album, *John Lennon/Plastic Ono Band*. The album had been greatly inspired by Lennon's experience of Dr. Arthur Janov's controversial Primal Scream therapy, and in recognition of that fact, Lennon assembled a collection of lyric drafts for

**below:** *Bob Dylan's draft lyrics for his classic 1966 song 'Just Like A Woman' sold for £6,325 ($9,487) in 1999.*

the album in booklet form. It was inscribed "to Art [Janov] and Vivian and all at number nine from John and Yoko and all at number 3", and dated 6 August 1970. The lyrics included one song that wasn't featured on the eventual album, "How", and also illustrated several variants from the words heard on the record. The sale price? $88,000 (around £58,650).

A year later at the same venue, a set of lyrics penned by Lennon for "If I Fell" realized $171,000 (£122,000), while a year earlier, in 1999, a single sheet of working lyrics for the Beatles' "I Am The Walrus", penned in black ink in Lennon's distinctive scrawl, sold for £78,500 (over $125,000) in London. Like a similar surviving manuscript for Paul McCartney's "Hey Jude", the handwriting stopped a verse or so before the eventual end of the song – suggesting in both cases that the initial stream of inspiration had run dry at that point, and that the rest of the song would require craftsmanship rather than genius to complete.

Those lyrics were obviously written out as a reference for the composer, to remind him of how far he had reached with the creation of his new song. But a songwriter might have many different reasons for setting his lyrics on paper. One set of McCartney lyrics for "Fool On The Hill" was written out on notepaper from the Hôtel Negresco in Nice, France. When they came up for auction they were extremely faded through age and exposure to sunlight, which clearly affected their value, but they were accompanied by a list of planned camera shots and angles, apparently in the hand of Beatles roadie Mal Evans. Both manuscripts dated from McCartney and Evans's lightning trip to France in autumn 1967, so that they could shoot a film clip to accompany "Fool On The Hill" in the *Magical Mystery Tour* movie. Evans needed the McCartney lyrics so that he could help to line up an appropriate shot for each line or section of the song.

How did these items reach the auction rooms? Often they were abandoned by their authors after their immediate use had expired, and left behind in recording studios, on film sets, or in office buildings. Some may even have been "rescued" from rubbish bins. This is one area where both moral and legal issues have to be satisfied before reputable auction houses will accept items for sale. There have been occasions when a songwriter has approached an auction house before a sale, and explained that the lyrics to a particular song had been stolen from them at some point in the past. If the seller's story doesn't stand up to scrutiny, then they may be politely requested to return the offending item, or face legal investigation. For many vendors, however, the chain of ownership has been clear-cut enough for them to be able to sell original Beatles manuscripts at auction. In the case of a lyric such as Paul McCartney's "Fool On The Hill", the words of the song may be familiar to millions of people around the world. But the fact that they exist in their composer's handwriting gives them a cachet beyond mere money.

The Beatles are far from being the only rock songwriters whose rough drafts are avidly sought after by well-heeled collectors. Bob Dylan is arguably the most revered composer of the rock era, and the most influential. Only a handful of his manuscripts have ever been offered for sale, including "Absolutely Sweet Marie" and "Just Like A Woman", all hailing from one of his most popular and highly regarded albums, *Blonde On Blonde*, and they have sold for between £4,000 and £7,000 apiece ($6,000 to $10,500). Bruce Springsteen, who early in his career was dogged by comparisons with Dylan, has also seen several manuscripts of early lyrics turn up at auction, notably the title track for his second album, *The E Street Shuffle*.

**above:** *Several Bruce Springsteen lyrics have surfaced at auction, such as this example for "The E Street Shuffle" from his second album.*

Three of rock's great lost talents have been represented more regularly at auction in this respect. Jim Morrison of the Doors was not only the man who wrote worldwide hit singles such as "Light My Fire" and "Riders On The Storm", but also a published poet in his own lifetime, now regarded as one of the most skilful and idiosyncratic wordsmiths of the rock era. In 1988, at a Christie's sale in New York, a mixture of Morrison's handwritten and typescript lyrics for his "Celebration of the Lizard" suite sold for $40,250 (£24,000).

Jimi Hendrix is still revered more than three decades after his death as the king of the rock guitar, but his own Dylan-inspired songwriting had a uniquely poetic touch. This has been well represented by the many drafts and lyric fragments that have come up for sale, such as the three-line fragment of lyrics for "Foxy Lady" that was sold in London in 1996 for £4,830 (around $7,000).

Marc Bolan may not have equalled the global impact of Morrison and Hendrix, but twenty-five years after his death he commands a loyal following, not only for his

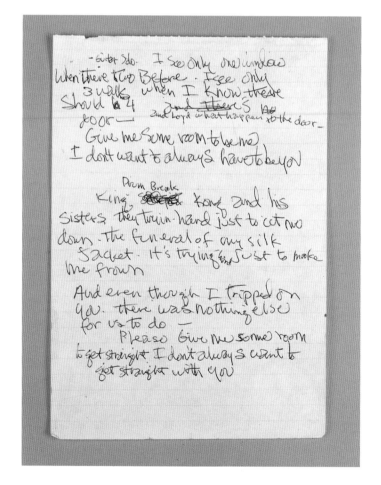

**right:** *Jimi Hendrix's lyrics for "Give Me Some Room", a song he wrote in the late 1960s but never recorded.*

glam-rock hits but for his "dungeons and dragons"-inspired brand of poetic whimsy. He was a notoriously bad speller, but examples of his verse and lyrics are snapped up by collectors.

Ironically, the worldwide publicity given to sales of these lyric sheets has probably encouraged most modern stars to take more care of their own manuscripts, to prevent them from coming up for auction in another twenty-five years' time. One exception to this rule was Lindsay Buckingham from Fleetwood Mac, as a large collection of lyric fragments, letters, doodles, set lists and other ephemera (even his chequebooks), all dating from Mac's commercial peak in the late 1970s, appeared on the market in 2000.

There have been precious few handwritten artefacts of any kind on the market from Madonna, Prince or Michael Jackson, however, which suggests that they have all become more aware of the possible implications of being too carefree with their work. Interestingly, some of the top acts of the 1960s, such as the Rolling Stones and the Who, have also not cropped up in this regard very often. Either they are excellent archivists, or else they made sure that when they'd finished with a lyric sheet, it was well and truly destroyed!

Maybe it's a sign of a devil-may-care attitude to his songwriting that several individual lyrics, and indeed an entire notebook of his work, by Oasis's Noel Gallagher have come up for auction. Looking through Gallagher's sheaf of lyrics is an almost surreal experience: here is a bunch of jottings and lyrics of the kind that you could probably find in any student household in the world. Yet amongst the false starts, personal reminders and set lists for concerts are the complete lyrics to million-selling singles such as "Roll With It".

For fans, collectors and historians, items such as the Gallagher notebook are of incredible interest. A similar example documented the songwriting career of the man often described as the father of country rock, Gram Parsons. Never a household name, since his death in 1973 at the age of twenty-six Parsons has become one of the most influential rock performers of all time, whose work has inspired everyone from 1970s stars such as the Eagles to the entire alternative country movement of recent years. The Parsons notebook was a particularly poignant item, as after his death it was passed to his sometime writing partner and close friend, the British musician Ric Grech. He continued to use it for his own songwriting efforts – until he in turn died prematurely, and the book came up at auction, selling for £3,300 ($4,770). Tantalizingly, its contents included many songs by both Parsons and Grech that were never recorded, and which are therefore lost to posterity, their melodies known to no-one.

The Gallagher and Parsons songwriting notebooks are one thing; but the ultimate rock collectible of all time would probably be the book in which two teenage songwriters from Liverpool, John Lennon and Paul McCartney, wrote out all their early songs. Under each lyric, they apparently wrote: "Another Lennon/McCartney Original". That must have seemed like adolescent boasting at the time, but the pair went on to become the most successful songwriters in history.

Paul McCartney has often referred in interviews to this elusive book, making comments like "I must have a look for it one day". Though it would be nice to think that the volume is still floating around Liverpool, waiting to be discovered, the chances are that it is sitting in the enormously well-guarded and completely secure McCartney archive, waiting for the day its owner opens a Beatles museum!

# A LETTER FROM BRIAN JONES

Brian Jones seems to have been the most prolific letter-writer in the Rolling Stones, single-handedly answering all queries that came his way. Indeed, at the very start of the Stones' career, Jones wrote one fan a letter that proved to have a lasting impact on his own life. The fan was one Doreen Pettifer, who had approached the Stones at a London club gig and offered to help get them some much-needed publicity. Besides writing to the BBC on their behalf, in the hope that the Stones might be rewarded with a radio session, Pettifer agreed to organize the first Rolling Stones Fan Club.

Consequently, in spring 1963, Brian Jones penned a nine-page letter to Pettifer detailing the band's formation, personnel and early history. It was intended as the basis of the Stones' first publicity handout, and snippets based on that letter continued to appear in media stories about the group for many years to come.

Utterly belying their later, rather arrogant reputation, Jones began the letter by telling Pettifer that "It's very gratifying that you should be so willing to help". Then he launched into his explanation of the group's history. He listed all six members, noting that "Bill Wyman, Bass, 23, works during the day as a storekeeper or something equally horrible. Only member of band married – only one who'll ever be married." Then he added, in an aside that betrayed the fact that Wyman had only been playing with the band for a matter of weeks at this point: "Proud father of a baby son (or daughter)".

The Stones would soon be world famous for the "offensive" length of their hair, but Jones told Pettifer: "Mick, Keith & myself, as I expect you noticed, wear our hair long, the others being more conventional". He explained that the Stones were "really an amalgamation of two bands. The one being an R&B band I formed about a year ago, & the other being a group run by Mick & Keith in S.E. London." He listed the regular gigs that the band played, and noted intriguingly: "We have signed an agreement with an independant [sic] recording company, I.B.C., who channel their releases through the major company labels. We have already cut quite a few sides, all on the commercial side." The nine pages of the letter are full of such titbits, all of which add significantly to our knowledge of the Rolling Stones' early career.

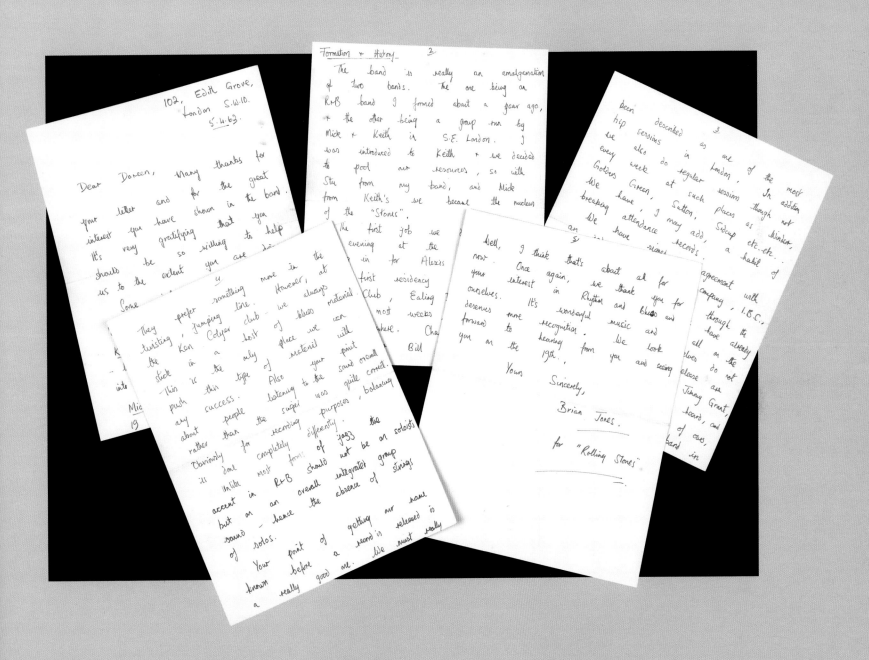

*chapter two*

RECORDINGS

**left:** *Elvis Presley and his Blue Moon Boys,*
*who effectively invented rock'n'roll with their*
*first recordings in 1954.*

Mankind has been making music since the dawn of time, yet for almost the whole of human history, you could only experience the performance of a musician if you were within earshot while he was playing. The invention of musical notation did at least allow musicians born thousands of miles, or even centuries, apart to perform the same music. But it is only in the last 100 years – a tiny fraction of humanity's lifetime on the earth – that it has become possible to document the exact sound of a performance for posterity.

Today, we take recording technology for granted, in all its different forms – CDs, DVDs, cassettes, digital tape, vinyl records, and maybe even a decaying pile of elderly 78rpm singles in the corner. In recent years manufacturers have introduced new formats with increasing rapidity; it seems that no sooner had we become used to compact discs, than the hi-fi industry was proclaiming that they would soon become obsolete.

Each new format is promoted as a dramatic improvement in sound quality and convenience over its predecessors; and just as certainly, each format that bites the dust has a hardcore of loyal supporters, who insist that recorded music will never sound the same again. The highly fragile 78rpm single, which was the standard currency of the recording industry until the late 1950s, was then pushed aside by the invention of microgroove technology – heard by the public on vinyl 33rpm LPs and 45rpm singles. These were much more difficult to break or damage than 78s had been, and in their 10" (25.5cm) or 12" (30.5cm) LP form, they allowed the listener to experience as much as twenty-five or thirty minutes at a sitting, before they had to turn the record over. But there is still a coterie of diehard rock'n'roll fans who say that the only way to hear Elvis Presley, Chuck Berry or Eddie Cochran is on an old 78.

Vinyl enjoyed more than two full decades of complete supremacy, through the 1960s and 1970s and well into the 1980s. This was the classic era of rock history, spanning everything from the Beatles to punk and disco, and from the Rolling Stones to the early years of Madonna and U2, so it's not surprising that vinyl artefacts have a tremendous nostalgic appeal to anyone who was buying records during those years. If you leave the question of sound quality aside, then there's no doubt that a 12"-square LP sleeve was a piece of art in its own right, and

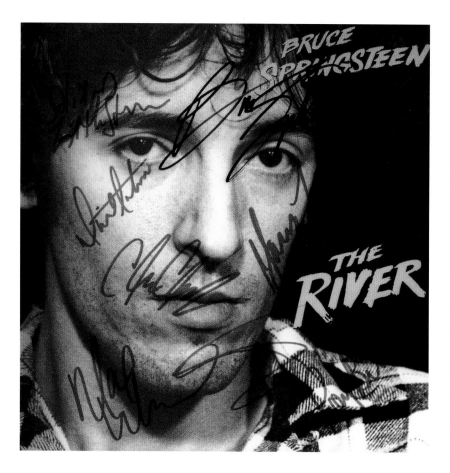

**below:** *Bruce Springsteen's* The River – *a best-selling record transformed into a collector's item by a set of autographs.*

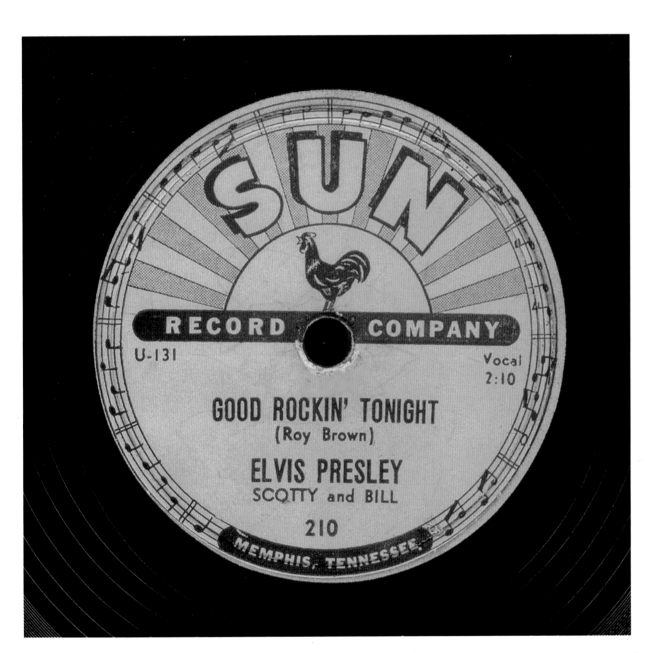

**above:** *One of the five seminal rockabilly singles recorded by Elvis Presley for the Sun label in Memphis during 1954 and 1955.*

**above:** *One of the most sought-after releases of the 1950s is this 10-inch LP from South Africa, teaming Elvis with Janis Martin, who was dubbed "the female Elvis Presley" by RCA.*

that nothing which has been introduced since then can match it for visual appeal.

In technological terms, though, CDs were greeted as being a real breakthrough when they became available to the mass market in the mid-1980s. Vinyl might not have been as delicate as the shellac from which 78s were made, but it still inevitably picked up wear and tear every time a record was played – or even pulled out of its sleeve. CDs instantly removed the scratches, clicks and background hiss that had been an intrinsic part of listening to recorded music since the start of the twentieth century. They were very difficult (though certainly not impossible) to damage, and in most cases they sounded just as good when they were played for the thousandth time as they had when they were brand-new. Once again, purists regarded progress as a backward step. There is still a minority of music-lovers who say that the digital sound of CDs (and all subsequent innovations, including minidiscs and DVDs) lacks the warmth and humanity of the analogue sound that was reproduced on 78s and vinyl.

Then there is the whole history of recording music on tape, from the cumbersome reel-to-reels that were the commercial standard until the early 1970s, through the era of the cassette, to the digital audio tape (DAT) of the 1990s – not forgetting sideroads like 8-track cartridges, which used to be fitted in millions of cars around the world, but now only survive in vintage American trucks.

All this means that the collector of recorded sound has an enormous amount of raw material to consider, presented in a confusing array of formats and sizes. As in most areas of pop and rock collecting, there is a market somewhere for almost anything. Having said that, 8-track cartridges usually sell for next to nothing, as novelty items more than anything else, simply because hardly

anyone still has the technology on which to play them. But there is a small band of devoted enthusiasts out there who are prepared to pay bafflingly huge prices for rare 8-track titles – if the recordings themselves are of historic interest – even though most collectors regard them as junk. For instance, an 8-track of any Beatles or Dylan album might appeal to diehard "completists" of their work.

The same applies to different musical styles and artists. Over the past two decades, the scope of the record collecting market has expanded almost beyond belief. At the start of the 1980s, which is when the market began to explode, helped by the birth of specialist magazines, record fairs and postal trading, ninety-nine per cent of collectors were interested in a few well-defined areas: the Beatles, Elvis Presley, the Rolling Stones and other stars of the 1950s–1970s; American rock'n'roll and rhythm & blues from the 1950s; British beat, R&B and psychedelia of the 1960s; 1960s soul; a small amount of 1970s progressive rock; and the pick of the limited edition punk and new wave artefacts through the 1970s and 1980s. Almost everything outside those areas could be picked up at rock-bottom prices.

Gradually, with every passing year, new genres and styles were added to the collectors' fare. There were surges of interest (and price rises) for reggae, blues, film soundtracks, post-punk, heavy metal and much more besides. By the mid-1990s, the collecting frenzy had reached those last bastions of the junkshops and charity stores – the easy listening albums. There was now no such thing as an uncollectible record: someone somewhere would want to collect it, and often the more kitsch and ridiculous it was, the better.

The early-to-mid-1990s also marked the peak of the vinyl collecting market. By then, sales of new vinyl releases had slumped to occupy only a few per cent of the market, while CDs took up the slack. Soon the cassette tape was also under threat, and sure enough by the end of the 1990s it had become difficult to find pre-recorded tapes for sale in anything smaller than a large city megastore. As the 1990s progressed, the average price of secondhand vinyl – com-mon items, in other words, that had no intrinsic value to collectors – slumped to almost nothing.

Yet vinyl remained alive and spinning in two significant areas. First of all, while the low-range material lost much of its value, the top end of the market continued to rise. Those records that were already established collector's items held their own through these turbulent times, despite the prophets of doom forecasting that the entire market was on the verge of collapse. As if to prove them wrong, vinyl unexpectedly began to claw its way back into the new-release and re-release market. A mixture of nostalgia, affection for LP artwork, demand from disc jockeys and respect for analogue sound combined to produce a demand for top-grade vinyl reissues of classic grooves from the past – particularly if they contained material that could be sampled by contemporary DJs and recording artists.

In collecting terms, it is actually the CD that has suffered most in recent years. While vinyl collectors avidly seek the first pressing of a desirable release, few if any people regarded CDs the same way. Only those items that contain exclusive material or were issued in very limited quantities have attracted prices to rival those of the top vinyl rarities.

Records are the biggest area of the pop and rock memorabilia market, but only occupy a small percentage of the time and space at the top auction houses. There is one very simple reason for this: the vast majority of secondhand records and CDs sell for less than £30 ($45), and therefore aren't worth selling at auction. As mentioned earlier, there are rarities that sell for much higher prices than that, but that wouldn't be considered by any international auction house, because their appeal and potential market are too selective.

To take one example, there are a handful of 1960s American soul singles that would fetch several thousand pounds apiece. But there is an equally small group of collectors who would be willing to pay those prices. They all know each other (even if their fierce rivalry sometimes means that they aren't speaking to each other!), and they usually buy, sell or trade these super-rare items within their own tight-knit community. A single such as Frank Wilson's "Do I Love You" (released in 1964, and one of the legendary US rarities from the Motown stable) would create an enormous stir amongst the soul community if it came up for sale, through a specialist record shop or collectors' magazine; but those same collectors probably wouldn't notice if a copy was offered at a London or New York auction house.

So for any record to qualify for a top auction, it has to satisfy three conditions: it has to be extremely rare and valuable, but with a big enough market potential, and it also has to carry some form of exclusivity and charisma. The select band of records that do make it to the auctioneer's hammer (in the metaphorical sense only, of course!) usually have a very special story to tell.

## ACETATES AND DEMOS

Perhaps the most exciting and tantalizing examples of rare records are acetates, which have effectively vanished from the recording industry in the modern age of compact discs. At first glance, acetates look identical to vinyl records – except that they are much thicker and heavier, and made out of more solid, inflexible lacquer material. They are designed to be played only a few times, and noticeably lose some of their sound quality much more quickly than ordinary vinyl records. Their attraction comes to collectors from the fact that they were individually cut, rather than mass-produced, and that they often contain material which never made it into the shops.

In the days before cassette recorders were widely available (i.e. before 1970), an acetate was often the only easy way for a recording artist, their producer or their manager to listen to the music that had just been recorded in the studio. The music was first recorded onto studio

master tapes – either entirely live, in the 1950s, or (as studio technology became more sophisticated in the 1960s and beyond) onto different "tracks" of a master-tape, which allowed two, four, eight, sixteen or more separate recordings of instruments and voices to be mixed (i.e. combined) into a finished master.

At any stage of the process, the recording engineer could document this work-in-progress by cutting an acetate disc. In the case of a group like the Beatles, the engineer might run off six or seven copies – one each for the group, one for their manager, Brian Epstein, another for producer George Martin, and so on. Sometimes only one copy would be cut; on other occasions, where the group wanted a number of journalists or disc jockeys to hear their new music "hot off the press", several dozen acetates might be prepared.

These acetates then served a variety of purposes. They allowed the artists to take a copy of their new recording home, and decide whether they thought it was satisfactory. They gave other members of the artists' entourage the opportunity to play the song to key press or radio contacts. Or they could be sent directly to the media, well in advance of the finished copies of the record being pressed for release through the shops.

Any acetate from the personal collection of a major artist would automatically have a cachet in its own right. Likewise, there is a keen market in acetates by the major pop and rock artists at auction. But the really big money is reserved for those

**left:** *No clues are evident on the label, but this is an unreleased Rolling Stones acetate from the mid-1960s.*

acetates that feature different recordings to the ones that eventually reached the public. These might be songs that were taped but then rejected for release; alternative takes of songs that did see the light of day in a different form; noticeably different mixes of well-known recordings; or versions that document an early stage of the recording process and lack many of the overdubs that were added later in the making of the record.

Particularly enticing to collectors was an acetate of the Beatles' "All You Need Is Love", which came up for auction in 2000. The song was a worldwide hit, of course, which went down in 1960s pop history as the British contribution to a global TV event entitled *Our World*. But this anthem of the psychedelic "summer of love" started life in an unusual fashion. When the Beatles cut the original backing track for the song on 14 June 1967, at Olympic Studios in Barnes, south-west London, they chose to use a very unorthodox collection of instruments. Just for this one recording, George Harrison played violin, Paul McCartney double bass and John Lennon harpsichord – plus the reliable Ringo Starr on drums.

At the end of the session, an acetate of the day's work was cut. It sounded nothing like the record that went around the world; in fact, anyone but a dedicated Beatles fan would find it a fairly excruciating listening experience. But that chaotic acetate, which ran for more than six-and-a-half minutes (three minutes longer than the finished record), is the only known documentary evidence of the preliminary stage of the recording process behind one of the Beatles' biggest hits, which is why it fetched a phenomenal £5,287 ($7,500) at auction.

The Beatles, and to a lesser extent the Rolling Stones, have dominated the acetate market at auctions. Even discs carrying identical versions of songs to those that reached

the shops have been snapped up. One of the unusual items that emerged was a 1969 copy of the Beatles' "Let It Be", pressed on an acetate from the Atlantic Recording Studios in New York. The Beatles never worked for Atlantic, or recorded in those studios; but the acetate was cut after representatives of the group had sent a tape of the newly written "Let It Be" to Atlantic's bosses, in the hope that Aretha Franklin might record it. Atlantic in turn transferred that tape onto an acetate, and another Beatles collectible was born – changing hands in 2001 for £5,875 ($8,225).

The better the story, the more demand there is for the artefact; and one Beatles acetate that attracted particular interest from collectors featured a song they wrote, but never issued themselves. The song was John Lennon's "Bad To Me", given to their stablemate in Brian Epstein's management organization, fellow Liverpool star Billy J. Kramer. The "Bad To Me" acetate turned out to be John's demo of the song, featuring his solo voice accompanied by himself and Paul McCartney on guitars. Kramer and his backing band, the Dakotas, used that very record to prepare their own version, a No. 1 hit in 1963. The label on the acetate, which sold for £2,937 ($4,400), credited Dick James Music Ltd., one of the companies owned by Lennon and McCartney's music publisher.

Precious acetates have also preserved for posterity recordings such as the original double-LP version of the Rolling Stones' live album *Get Yer Ya-Ya's Out*. The original live tapes on these acetates were heavily overdubbed in the studio before the album was released (as a single LP), and so once again the acetate had an extra importance because it documented material that would otherwise have been lost forever. For collectors, this Stones item was made all the more attractive because it carried custom labels from the Beatles' Apple Studios in London, which is where the recordings were assembled, given a rough mix, and then transferred onto acetate.

Some acetates are highly collectible; and all Beatles and Rolling Stones acetates are very sought after. But it would be a mistake to imagine that every acetate actually represents a potential goldmine. There are thousands of acetates in existence by unknown or obscure artists that might have some degree of interest to specialist collectors, but which would never be offered at auction. As usual, it's the combination of celebrity and exclusivity that brings the richest rewards.

Acetates are often linked with demos – one of the most confusing areas of record collection. "Demos" is short for demonstration discs, but that can cover a multitude of different items. As in the case of John Lennon's "Bad To Me", an acetate could qualify as a demo if it was demonstrating a new song. More often, record companies would press a small quantity – sometimes a handful, sometimes several hundred – of demo copies of a new or forthcoming release that would be handed out to the media. These were often known as "white labels", because they would come with a plain white label in place of the usual company design, with the track details handwritten or typed instead of printed. (More confusion beckons there, because acetates usually carry exactly the same kind of "white label", again with handwritten details.)

From the 1950s until the 1970s, the major record companies usually printed special white "demo" labels for the copies they sent out to the press – often with a large "A" overprinted on the side of the single that they were keen to promote. These singles are sometimes known as "A labels", for obvious reasons; or "promos", a more inclusive term that covers any record sent out by the com-

pany to promote a new release, many of which may look identical to the copies in the shops.

Fortunately, at least as far as the auction market is concerned, "demos", "white labels", "promos" and the rest rarely attain the rarity values that the top auction houses require for their lots. The major exception, inevitably, is the Beatles, where almost all of their 1960s "A label" demos will sell for several hundred pounds (or dollars) apiece, and the first ("Love Me Do") can reach a four-figure sum. "Love Me Do" is of particular interest, because it dates from a time when EMI could misspell one of the Beatles' surnames as "McArtrey' – and no-one noticed the mistake!

## STUDIO TAPES

As acetates that preserve different stages of the recording process can be highly collectible, it seems obvious that the studio master tapes on which music is originally recorded ought to be even more desirable. Yet for two main reasons, studio tapes have rarely made a major impression on the auction scene.

The first and most important drawback to selling master tapes is the problem of ownership. Acetates were given to a variety of people in the music business, but almost all studio tapes remain the property of the record company that made them. In the case of the Beatles, for example, there would theoretically be enormous interest from collectors if a master tape of "All You Need Is Love" came onto the market. But there would be even greater interest from the copyright holders of the tape, EMI Records, who would quite rightly want to reclaim property that is legally theirs.

The second difficulty is a technical one. Anyone who has a CD player can play a CD; likewise with vinyl or cassette tapes. But studio master tapes come in a bewildering variety of different sizes (both the diameter of the reel and the actual width of the tape can vary), speeds (expressed in i.p.s., or inches per second) and formats (a 4-track tape won't play on a 2-track machine, and vice versa). When record companies remaster vintage material from decades-old master tapes, their biggest problem is often locating the right playback equipment for each reel. Very few individual collectors own the studio facilities to enable them to make any use of these master tapes.

**below:** *The earliest known tape of Mick Jagger and Keith Richards playing in a friend's bedroom went under the hammer for £50,250 ($75,375).*

Some items have made it into top auctions despite these potential problems. When a record company or recording studio went out of business in the 1960s or 1970s, its master tapes often ended up being thrown out or mislaid. In one legendary instance, the entire tape archive of one of London's most famous recording studios of the 1960s was discovered sitting in a rubbish skip, ready to be destroyed, when the buildings were being refurbished. The contractor in charge of the site apparently passed the tapes onto a collector for a nominal sum; and as a result, masters by artists such as the Who, the Rolling Stones and Eric Clapton began to filter onto the

collector's market. But despite their fascinating contents, and the outlandish story behind their discovery, their prices at auction were disappointing – simply because collectors weren't willing to shell out for tapes that they knew they would never be able to play.

One important point in all this regards copyright – ownership of which entitles a company or person to make commercial use of the recordings. Except in very extreme circumstances (for instance, if the assets of a bankrupt company were being auctioned), studio tapes are never sold with copyright. You may own the actual piece of tape on which the Rolling Stones originally recorded one of their 1960s classics; but that doesn't give you any legal right to turn the tape into a CD or a record, or make any kind of commercial copy of its contents. With copyright, a Stones tape could be worth a small fortune; without copyright, it would probably struggle to reach £300 ($450) or so.

## INTERVIEWS

Musical copyright is one thing; copyright in the spoken word is something else entirely. The difference provides a loophole whereby original tapes of interviews conducted by press or radio journalists with star performers can be sold at auction for often astronomical sums.

Copyright law obviously differs in detail around the world, but it's standard practice that record companies only own the musical copyright in their performers' work, not the copyright in their speech. As usual, the Beatles provide the most illuminating example. The copyright in every note the Beatles played and recorded, in public or private, between September 1962 (when they signed to Parlophone Records) and their split in spring 1970 is controlled by EMI Records, no matter who

owns the actual tape or disc on which it is recorded. But the copyright in any interviews with the Beatles recorded during that period belongs to the person who made the recording – or who paid for it to be made. That may be the interviewer, or their radio station, TV station or newspaper owner. In all of these cases, the Beatles themselves have no control over what is done with the tape.

That situation has altered somewhat these days, as many major stars now insist that all interviewers sign a contract – the showbiz equivalent of a pre-nuptial agreement – pledging that they will only use the material they record for the agreed magazine or TV show, and that ultimate copyright resides with the artist, not the interviewer. If you don't sign, you don't get the interview.

**below:** *Several crucial tapes of recordings by the late Jimi Hendrix have surfaced in recent years, arousing speculation about what other treasures may still be awaiting discovery.*

Nobody was thinking that way back in the 1960s, however, with the result that a handful of lucky interviewers have been able to sell tapes of their conversations with the Beatles, Elvis Presley or other superstars for very handsome sums. For example, in the summer of 1971 an Australian journalist was invited by Yoko Ono to the Lennons' home, Tittenhurst Park in Berkshire, England, ostensibly to interview Yoko about her book, *Grapefruit*. However, inspired by an enthusiastic and perceptive interviewer, John and Yoko provided some of their most revealing comments on the nature of creativity and the unique nature of Yoko's work. Competitive bidding resulted in a final price of £23,500 ($35,000) when the tape was sold at Christie's London saleroom in April 2002. However, this is very much the exception, and to date no press or radio interview tapes recorded after 1971 have achieved a notable price at auction.

## BOOTLEGS/PRIVATE RECORDINGS

With very few exceptions (the Grateful Dead are the most significant example), pop and rock performers don't encourage their fans to tape their live concerts, even for their own personal use. Their fear is that these illicit tapes will be turned into "bootlegs" – underground LPs, CDs or cassettes featuring rare or unissued material by major artists that are avidly collected by fans, but strictly illegal to manufacture, distribute or sell. Any auction house that sells a bootleg recording is simply revealing its lack of knowledge – and, indeed, risking legal action.

Yet there is a select number of private recordings by major artists that have made a major impact on the auction market – and where any possible legal complications have been massively outweighed by the enormous historical value of the recordings.

It won't surprise anyone who has read this far to discover that the two most valuable items relate to the Beatles and the Rolling Stones. In July 1957, sixteen-year-old John Lennon's skiffle and rock'n'roll group, the Quarry Men, performed at a church fête in Liverpool. Later that day, he was introduced by his friend Ivan Vaughan to a younger boy who also played guitar – Paul McCartney. This was the first meeting of the two men who would eventually become recognized as the most successful songwriting partnership in history.

It is almost unbelievable, but someone with an interest in sound recording was in the audience for that Quarry Men performance, and he taped a few minutes of their set, capturing two songs – "Puttin' On The Style" and "Baby Let's Play House". Even more incredibly, he kept the tape without realizing exactly what he had documented.

More than thirty-five years later in 1994, that unique and historic six-minute recording was offered for sale, complete with the machine on which it had been taped; and it sold for £78,500 ($117,000). The sound quality of the recording was primitive, to say the least, and Lennon's voice was scarcely recognizable, but its value to posterity as a document of an historic day is beyond price.

The Rolling Stones tape is slightly different, in that the artists did at least know that they were being recorded. Not that they were known as the Rolling Stones when a college friend taped them running through a set of rhythm & blues songs in his bedroom in early 1962. The band were then known as Little Boy Blue & the Blue Boys, but only two of the eventual Stones line-up, Mick Jagger and Keith Richards, were members of that group.

The bedroom tape proved to be the earliest surviving recording of any Stones-related line-up – and what gave it much of its appeal to a well-heeled collector was its remarkably good sound quality, matched by its naïve but enthusiastic musical skill. It demonstrated that any group featuring Jagger and Richards, no matter how young, was going to sound like the Rolling Stones. It also filled in a vital early chapter in the group's history, with an immediacy that no written account could match. The only sad part of the story is that the sound quality, although good by early 1960s home recording standards, rendered it unsuitable for commercial release, as Stones fans would have relished the opportunity to hear their idols at such a formative stage. It currently resides in a private collection.

What gave both of these tapes their financial and historical value was the unique nature of their contents. No doubt there are thousands of similar tapes in existence documenting budding 1950s and 1960s performers who never made it onto any ladder of stardom. Sadly, they only have curiosity value. Even more sad is the knowledge of what has been lost down the years, through carelessness or bad luck. After those two tapes were sold, several other individuals emerged with tales of what might have been – recordings of the early Beatles or Stones that were wiped clean to tape an inconsequential programme off the radio, or simply thrown away in the belief that they were of no financial value. What's tantalizing is the thought that there may still be similar items hidden away in dusty cupboards or lofts – tapes of Elvis Presley or Bob Dylan performing at their high school concerts, the

Who's first rehearsal sessions in a west London club, or a sound-check by Blondie's Debbie Harry when she was still with the all-girl group the Stilletoes. Collectors never give up hope of locating another fragment of the Holy Grail.

**right:** *Unreleased acetates and tapes by the Who (pictured here in 1966) have often attracted high prices at auction.*

## RARE RECORDS

The British magazine *Record Collector* publishes a bi-annual *Rare Record Price Guide* that lists the current values of more than 100,000 records, tapes and CDs issued between 1950 and the present day. Similar guides are published in the USA, Germany, Japan and no doubt many other countries as well. The market for rare and collectible records is endless.

As mentioned, only a miniscule proportion of these rarities would ever be offered for sale by a top auction house. There is a well-established network of shops, fairs, postal auctions and internet sites that handles the other 99.9 per cent of the record collecting market.

**opposite:** *The most valuable punk record ever released: the A&M edition of "God Save The Queen". A copy sold for £3,760 ($5,600) in 2002.*

To qualify for an auction slot in London or New York, rare records don't simply have to be valuable; they have to be legendary. No collectible record has a more famous or gripping tale behind it than the Beatles' "butcher cover" – or, as it is more prosaically if accurately known, the first version of their American-only LP, *Yesterday And Today*.

As its title suggests, the album was built around Paul McCartney's song "Yesterday". In Britain, that number appeared on the *Help!* film soundtrack album, but to the group's disgust, their US record company, Capitol Records, chose to butcher the contents of their early UK albums, cutting a couple of tracks from each one and then adding in singles that weren't included on the original LPs. As a result, they were able to flood the market with exclusive American albums, over which the Beatles had no control.

When the group was requested to provide cover artwork for *Yesterday And Today*, they collaborated with photographer Robert Freeman to produce a picture that reflected their view of Capitol Records' tactics. They posed in butchers' aprons, streaked with blood, clutching slabs of raw meat and mutilated dolls. It was the complete antithesis of a normal record company promotional photograph in 1966 – and it's proof of the power the Beatles wielded at that point that Capitol actually agreed to print the first run of album covers using that photograph.

When copies began to leak out to the American media, the photograph was greeted with a degree of outrage, bordering on hysteria. (Intriguingly, the same photograph was used in Britain to promote the "Paperback Writer" single, causing no comment at all.) Fearing a storm of adverse publicity that could blight sales of the album, Capitol's executives took the decision to withdraw the offending cover, just three days before the record was due to appear in the shops.

Over the intervening weekend, all available Capitol staff were recruited to take the "butcher" sleeves, and paste a much blander photograph over the top. The new cover showed a very bored group of Beatles posing around a suitcase or trunk; and so the "trunk cover" and the "butcher cover" passed into collectors' lore.

Remarkably, tens of thousands of "trunk covers" were prepared by hand that weekend, and rushed into the stores. All subsequent printings of the sleeve used the new "trunk" artwork. But enough copies of the original "butcher" sleeve had already passed into circulation for the legend to grow – and grow. By the early 1970s, the "butcher cover" was already renowned as America's top Beatles rarity. It remains so today, even though there are other items from the US that actually attract higher prices. But no serious collection of Beatles memorabilia can be considered complete without a "butcher cover".

This sought-after sleeve exists in three different forms, or "states". The first state is the most desirable of all: it features the original artwork, without the new cover pasted on top. The second state does have the "trunk cover", but with traces of the "butcher" artwork just visible underneath (check alongside Ringo Starr's left arm to see if it's there). That's also known as the "unpeeled cover". The third state is known as the "peeled cover", because it is a copy on which the "trunk cover" has been peeled, ripped or steamed off, to display the "butcher" design underneath. This is virtually impossible to do without tearing the original cover, so "peeled" sleeves usually show large signs of damage.

All three states of the "butcher cover" are of huge interest to collectors, with condition being very important. But the "trunk cover" (without the "butcher" underneath) was manufactured in enormous quantities, running into several million, and has no great financial value.

Another classic rarity that was created by notoriety and outrage was the Sex Pistols' "God Save The Queen" single. More than twenty-five years after the event, it's difficult for anyone who wasn't around at the time to imagine the widely felt disgust aroused in Britain by the Sex Pistols and the punk movement they led. Newspapers competed to print ever more shocking stories about their antics; and a prominent TV interviewer lost his job after he encouraged members of the group to swear during a live show.

The Sex Pistols were dropped by their first record label, EMI, after one single, "Anarchy In The UK", because the company no longer wished to be associated with such a controversial band. They moved to A&M Records, who agreed to issue their second single, "God Save The Queen" – neatly timed to coincide with Queen Elizabeth II's Silver Jubilee in 1977. What exactly happened next is still being debated, decades later, but A&M executives came under pressure from other artists on the label to terminate the Pistols' contract. This they did, but only after pressing up the initial run of "God Save The Queen" singles. The vast majority of these were destroyed, but a handful slipped out. Within a few weeks, these were changing hands for more than £50 (then about $75), at a time when a new single only cost £1 ($1.50); and today they can fetch well over £2,000 ($3,000).

The story didn't end there. "God Save The Queen" was immediately picked up by the less timid Virgin label and

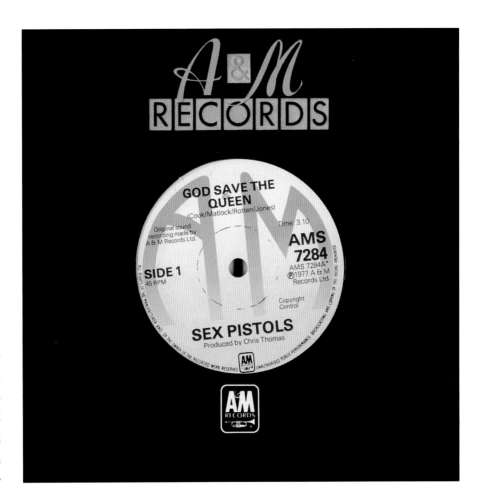

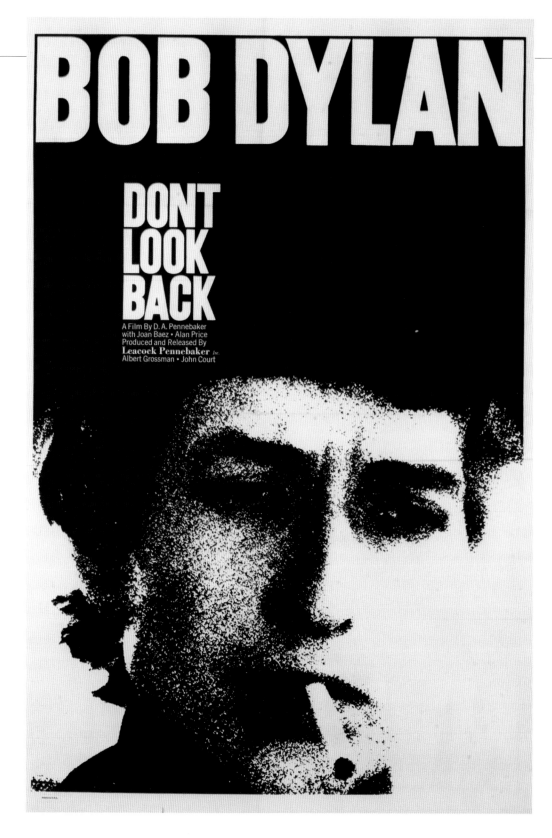

**right:** *This US poster for Bob Dylan's Dont Look Back [sic] documentary film fetched £700 ($1,050) at a London auction in 2000.*

became a massive hit record in the UK. Contrary to popular belief, Virgin copies of the single are worth only a few pounds. More than two decades later, A&M folded as an independent label, and was enveloped by the multi-national Universal group. As a gesture to their loyal staff, A&M executives opened up the last surviving box of "God Save The Queen" singles, and gave their employees one each as a leaving present. This virtually doubled the number of copies in circulation overnight, and has helped to stabilize (but not noticeably reduce) the value of these A&M rarities.

Few rare records have quite such colourful histories as *Yesterday And Today* and "God Save The Queen". But there are a select number of collectible items by an elite cast-list – the Beatles, Elvis Presley, the Rolling Stones, Madonna, David Bowie, etc. – of sufficient stature and value to qualify for the auction houses. These include the five original Sun singles Elvis Presley recorded in 1954 and 1955; the earliest 45rpm singles by Bowie, issued under the name of Davie Jones & the Kingbees or the Manish Boys in the mid-1960s; withdrawn items by the Rolling Stones (such as the "Poison Ivy" single, with-drawn just before release in 1963) and Madonna (the "Erotica" 12" picture disc, also pulled from the shops because of its risqué imagery); and an array of Beatles items, ranging from limited edition red vinyl pressings from Japan of their albums, to rare editions of some of their earliest US albums. None of them, however, will impress your friends as much as a "butcher cover" or an A&M "God Save The Queen".

## FILMS

Like their aural counterparts, rare films of rock's premier superstars can provide the only known documentation of significant events in their careers. Few such items have ever come up for sale at auction, because of a familiar stumbling block – copyright ownership. As with tapes, there is also the potential problem that a purchaser needs the right equipment to view the film, and few people in the era of video and digital tape have their own 8mm or 16mm screening facilities.

The major items that have come onto the market in recent years have all been related to the Beatles – and usually to the filming in autumn 1967 of their *Magical Mystery Tour* movie. The Beatles spent a couple of weeks in the West Country while they were making the film, working in public places where they could easily be glimpsed by fans. Many of them captured the events on cine film, and choice examples have come up for sale.

More interesting still have been collections of home-movie footage taken by friends and associates of the Beatles, including their 1960s road manager, the late Mal Evans. With his unique access to the group, he was able to shoot them on vacation and in other surroundings that were barred to professional film-makers and TV crews. Like the *Magical Mystery Tour* cine films, however, his reels were always shot without sound, making them fascinating but also frustrating items to view.

What the auction market needs, in order to establish film of pop and rock stars as an important area, is for someone to turn up a really sensational piece of footage – sound-and-vision documentary clips of the early Beatles or Rolling Stones, for example. However, such has been the publicity given to both groups over the last forty years, one has to assume that any such footage would have been exhumed long before now.

# LOST SONGS ON ACETATE

It is often the case that recordings which were never released to the public have only survived on acetate records. For example, Marc Bolan (the future leader of UK glam-rock icons T. Rex) taped four songs at Decca Studios in London late in 1965, in the very early stages of his career, in the hope that one of them would prove to be suitable for release as his second single. In the event, not one of the tunes – "Song For A Soldier", "Reality", "Highways" and "Rings Of Fortune" – was regarded as being a likely hit, and he returned to Decca early the next year with another batch of material. Down the years, Decca wiped or lost the master tape of this session; and it was only in 2002 that individual acetates of the four songs were located by Christie's, from the collection of Bolan's producer at the time, the late Mike Leander, and offered up for sale. No other copies of those songs are known to exist.

According to the British magazine *Record Collector*, the most valuable acetate in the world features the first two studio recordings by the Quarry Men – the Liverpool skiffle and rock'n'roll group who became rather better known as the Beatles. In early summer 1958, the Quarry Men line-up of Lennon, McCartney, Harrison, Colin Hanton and John "Duff" Lowe went into Percy Phillips' recording studio in Liverpool and cut two songs: the Buddy Holly hit "That'll Be The Day" and the McCartney/Harrison composition "In Spite Of All The Danger". They emerged with an acetate copy of the songs, which they agreed to share amongst the group – each member keeping it for a few months at a time. But they soon forgot about its existence, and it ended up in the collection of John "Duff" Lowe.

In theory, this artefact would fetch well over £100,000 (more than $150,000) if it ever came up for auction today. But there's a catch: Lowe sold it to none other than Paul McCartney, and it's impossible to imagine a situation in which he would agree to sell it. Instead, he pressed up a small quantity of reproductions of the single, some playing at 45rpm and some at 78rpm, and sent them to friends as a Christmas present. Not even these copies have ever been offered for sale; the first person who does break ranks is likely to vanish from the McCartney Christmas card list very quickly!

*chapter three*

# GUITARS AND OTHER INSTRUMENTS

**left:** *Eric Clapton playing his legendary*
*1956 Fender Stratocaster guitar, which he*
*nicknamed "Brownie".*

Instruments are the raw material of the music industry; without them none of what Joni Mitchell once called "the star-making machinery behind the popular song" would ever take shape. Besides providing the sound for fifty years of rock'n'roll music, guitars (and, to a lesser extent, drums) have become a key visual element of pop culture. There's a good reason why generations of youngsters have posed in front of their bedroom mirror clutching a tennis racket and pretending they were playing guitar like Eric Clapton, Jimi Hendrix or Kurt Cobain – guitars, especially electric guitars, have a "cool"

*below: Instruments with a particular personal association, like Rolling Stone Brian Jones' "teardrop" guitar, are very collectible.*

factor that seems destined to survive as long as rock music itself. At various times over the last few decades, contemporary pop has drifted away from guitar-based groups and songs towards the synthesiser-based sounds of the 1980s, for instance, or the DJ and sampling culture of the 1990s. But no matter what kind of modern technology is at musicians' disposal, rock music always seems to return to the guitar. The same principle applies to auctions, where other instruments only come up for sale if they have a personal association with a major artist.

Certain makes and models of guitar have acquired "classic" status, and attracted a keen collector's market of

their own. Like records, collectible guitars have an established hierarchy away from the mainstream auction market, and in both fields it can take a lifetime to master all the details. Guitar specialists can spend hours discussing the minutiae of pick-ups, rotary controls, machine heads and bridges, not to mention serial numbers, modifications and hybrids. But without assuming expert status, it's possible to have a working knowledge of what instruments are likely to attract the attention of collectors, and why.

Besides those instruments that have an inherent rarity value in themselves, the other models that often crop up at auction are those that have been signed, owned or used by leading rock stars. Guitars of no particular value to the collector (or, indeed, the musician) may fetch a good price if they were once the proud possession of a teenage Beatle or Rolling Stone. Even such insignificant accessories as drumsticks or guitar pickguards turn into collector's items with the right signature attached. As George Harrison complained jokingly in the early 1980s in a letter to a friend, "An acoustic guitar of mine was auctioned for £3,000 (over $4,500) – and that was for a guitar I only owned for ten minutes!"

Of course, the ultimate six-string collectible would be a sought-after instrument in its own right that also once belonged to a star name. More than 100 items that comfortably satisfied both criteria were auctioned at Christie's New York saleroom in June 1999, during the most important rock guitar sale ever staged.

The event was the auction of part of Eric Clapton's extensive collection of guitars, both vintage and contemporary, to raise money for a cause very close to his heart. The beneficiary was the Crossroads Centre for drug rehabilitation, which Clapton had recently helped to establish

**left:** *When Eric Clapton's "Brownie" guitar was sold at Christie's in 1999, it fetched a remarkable $497,500 (£311,000).*

in Antigua. In the catalogue for the sale, Clapton admitted: "It wasn't my idea to sell these guitars, it was suggested by a friend who thought it would be a good way to illustrate my commitment to 'Crossroads Antigua', and also raise money and awareness for the centre at the same time . . . The guitars themselves represent the journey I have made through music over the last four decades of my life, they reflect my tastes in music, and sometimes the heroes I have tried so hard to emulate."

*right: Another Fender Strat from the Clapton collection: he gave this example to his bodyguard, who later sold it at auction.*

In a much earlier interview, Clapton summed up the qualities that would make his auction so irresistible: "If you can pick up a guitar and tell that someone great has played it – you can actually tell that – then you want to take it and endow yourself with what the guitar's got."

The star item at the sale was the guitar known as "Brownie" – one of two individually named Fender Stratocasters (the other is called "Blackie", and remains in Clapton's possession) that have passed into legend in his hands. "Brownie" was a 1956 Stratocaster with a sunburst finish, which he had bought from the London shop Sound City back in May 1967 when he was a member of the psyche-delic blues-rock group Cream. Back

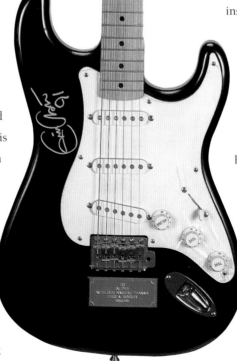

then, he paid £150 (which was almost $300) for the guitar; in 1999, it sold for $497,500 (£310,950). What happened in between was that Clapton used this instrument to record perhaps his most popular and celebrated song: "Layla". It could be seen on the back cover of his Derek & the Dominos album, *Layla And Other Assorted Love Songs*; and he was also pictured holding the instrument on the front cover of his earlier solo album, simply titled *Eric Clapton*. "I've been very fortunate to play hundreds of Strats over the years," he explained before the sale, "but that one, for some reason, just had something."

Along with the Gibson Les Paul, the Fender Stratocaster has become synonymous with the rock guitar, and with Clapton in particular. His Crossroads sale included many fine examples of the instrument, including one which dated from 1954, the year that this model was introduced. Like all Strats, it carried a serial number, and it also showed evidence of its date of manufacture, with the legend "T-G-9-54" pencilled along the neck by a Fender employee. (Incidentally, it is quite possible for the same instrument to carry slightly different dates on its neck and body.) Clapton found it ideal for playing slide guitar, which is one of the qualities that gives it a normal price range of $20,000–$30,000 (£14,000–£21,000), even without any association with fame.

At the Crossroads sale, however, this instrument raised the remarkable price of $211,500, which is over £130,000.

Around 1958, Fender began to manufacture custom versions of the Stratocaster, and one famous brand – with translucent blonde finish and gold-plated metal parts – became known as "Mary Kayes", after the name of a musician and bandleader who appeared in trade ads at that time. "It has a jazz feel to it that makes it difficult to play blues on," Clapton said of his "Mary Kaye", "but it's ideal for recording work." In fine condition, such a model could sell for £20,000–£25,000 (or between $30,000 and $37,500) today – or, with the Clapton connection, £45,000 ($67,500).

The Stratocaster continued to be manufactured right through the "classic" rock era, from the mid-1950s and into the early 1970s. But connoisseurs usually prefer to concentrate on instruments made before 1966. That's because Fender was bought out by the CBS corporation in January 1965, and within a few months certain elements of the production process had been streamlined. The result, as far as the experts are concerned, is that the post-1966 instruments simply don't sound as good as their earlier counterparts.

Despite that, one of the highest prices ever paid for a Fender Stratocaster was raised by a model manufactured in March 1968. At a London auction in April 1990, this guitar sold for an incredible £198,000 ($316,800). Why? Because it came from the collection of Jimi Hendrix's long-time drummer, Mitch Mitchell, and proved to have been the instrument Hendrix used at the Woodstock festival in 1969. That was the occasion when he performed a particularly tortured rendition of "The Star Spangled Banner", which has passed into rock legend as a direct comment by the guitarist on the sorry state of America during the turmoil of the civil rights struggle and the Vietnam War. It's one of the most celebrated guitar solos in history, so it's not surprising that the instrument that was used to produce such astounding music should attract an equally breathtaking price.

*left: Paul McCartney signed this 1990s Fender Squier Stratocaster guitar so that it could be sold for charity.*

In 1979, Fender celebrated the twenty-fifth birthday of the Strat with a special anniversary edition (incidentally, Clapton was presented with no. 000002). These models now sell for £3,000–£4,000 ($4,500–6,000), as do the Stratocaster Elites – designed with a 1950s-style neck and a "Mary Kaye"-style cream finish, and first put on the market in 1983. The early 1980s also saw Fender introduce a reissue of the 1957 Stratocaster design, which has become a collector's item itself; while Clapton's auction also featured a Stratocaster XII (a twelve-string

model) with a standard price tag today of £4,000–£5,000 ($6,000–$7,500). His model, of course, fetched an even more impressive $48,300 (£32,000). More recently, a fortieth anniversary Stratocaster was produced in 1994, in a run of (appropriately) just forty copies.

Given Clapton's long-standing connection with this guitar, it's not surprising that Fender also suggested the idea of manufacturing an Eric Clapton Signature Stratocaster. Three prototypes were made in 1986, and presented to Clapton. Two were finished in pewter (apparently to match his Mercedes!), while he handed on the third, which was finished in red, to England cricket star Ian Botham, in return for one of his bats. Botham had better take care of his gift: one of Clapton's pewter pair sold for $107,000 (£67,000) at the Crossroads sale.

The Eric Clapton Signature model went into commercial production in 1988, featuring a facsimile of the guitarist's autograph at the very top of the neck. In 1990, a second signature model was added to the series, named "Blackie" after the 1950s black composite model that remains one of Clapton's favourite instruments. Various customized finishes have been prepared for the Signature guitars, spanning everything from "Mary Kaye" cream to a garish green that Clapton dubbed "7-Up"!

Before Fender developed the Stratocaster, the California-based company had established itself in 1950 with an electric Spanish guitar named the Esquire. Later that year, the Fender Broadcaster joined their range; and

*right: This custom-made Cloud solid body guitar is associated with Prince at the height of his fame in the 1980s. It sold for £11,000 ($16,500) in 1993.*

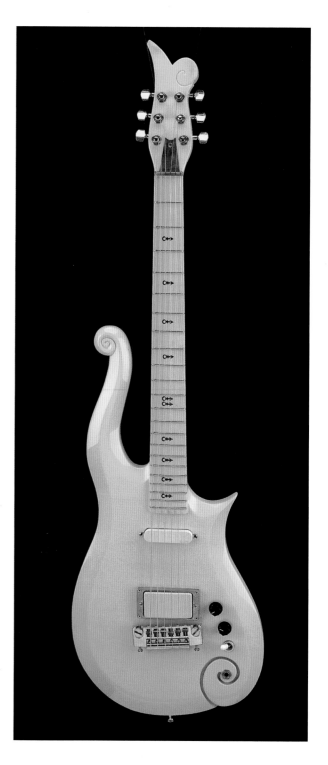

during 1951, the Broadcaster was renamed the Telecaster, another guitar with a long and illustrious rock history. It lost out to the "Strat", which appeared in 1954, in the long term, because the latter was more versatile – it had three pick-ups and rotary controls, as against the Telecaster's two of each, plus the attraction of a five-way selector switch. But early versions of the Telecaster can fetch £8,000–£12,000 ($12,000–$18,000), while even 1970s instruments could sell for £3,000–£4,000 ($4,500–$6,000). Once again, there was a fortieth anniversary edition, marketed in a run of 300 in 1992. In fact, the run actually extended to 301, as Eric Clapton expressed interest in having one of these models just after the edition had sold out, so Fender manufactured an extra guitar for him, numbered "000". That sold for $70,700 (about £45,000) in New York, but was out-classed by Clapton's original 1952 Telecaster, which was sold for $101,500 (nearly £64,000).

Other Fender guitars from their most sought-after era of the 1950s and early 1960s include the Jazzmaster, which proved popular with many US garage bands, and the Jaguar. Bass players, meanwhile, often single out the Fender Precision as one of the finest instruments that has ever been manufactured.

In Clapton's eyes, the only rival to the Fender Strat would probably be the Gibson Les Paul, a signature model named after a pioneer of the recording industry who was also a guitar virtuoso in his own right. "When I get up there on stage," Clapton once reflected, "I often go through a great deal of indecision, even while I'm playing. If I've got a black Stratocaster on, and I'm in the middle of a blues, I am kind of going, 'Aw, I wish I had the Les Paul'. Then again, if I were playing the Les Paul, the sound would be great, but I'd be going, 'Man, I wish I had the

Stratocaster neck'. I'm always caught in the middle of those two guitars."

The Gibson Les Paul Model was introduced in 1952; two years later, Gibson added the Les Paul Custom to their range, while in 1961 the tremolo-armed SG Les

**above:** *This Japanese custom-shaped Coyote guitar, signed by ZZ Top, fetched £1,400 ($1,700) at Christie's first rock sale in 1985.*

**below:** *One of the most valuable guitars ever*
*sold: the Gibson Super 400C was used by*
*Elvis Presley in the 1950s and also in 1969.*

Paul Standard and vibrato-free Les Paul Junior took the place of the original model. In one or more of these forms, the Les Paul became associated with a glorious generation of 1960s British guitarists, including Jimmy Page, Jeff Beck, Keith Richards, George Harrison and, of course, Clapton himself. Individual 1950s instruments have sold for as much as £18,000 ($27,000), but a more standard price would be £8,000 ($12,000), or slightly less for a 1960s model. In 2000, a Les Paul Standard from 1958, which had been bought by Eric Clapton in 1968 and then passed on to Paul Kossoff of Free, sold for £47,000 ($70,000).

The Les Paul guitars form only part of Gibson's rich heritage, however. The company was the first to manufacture archtop guitars in the 1930s, while legendary pre-war bluesmen such as Robert Johnson often used early Gibson models such as the L-1 or L-3 (both acoustic, of course). The L-5 model has long been a collector's favourite, while another Gibson landmark was the ES-150, the company's first electric guitar, introduced in 1936. Both the ES-150 and the slightly later ES-250 were used by jazz guitar legend Charlie Christian, which is a good enough recommendation for any would-be collector. But there are many other sought-after Gibson models from the pre-rock'n'roll era, such as the Super 400C, the

ES-125 and the mid-1950s model, the Byrdland, which can fetch more than £10,000 ($15,000) at auction.

The most valuable example of the Super 400C to have been sold at auction was a mid-1950s model, purchased on 8 January 1957 by Scotty Moore. As rock'n'roll scholars will know, Moore was the guitarist who accompanied Elvis Presley on his meteoric ascent from obscurity to superstardom between 1954 and 1956, and he played this particular Gibson on such memorable hit records as "All Shook Up", "Jailhouse Rock" and "One Night (With You)". It can also be seen in the movies Elvis made during the late 1950s.

Elvis often picked up the guitar and played it during that period, and he had a second opportunity to mess with the instrument in 1969. By then, Moore had sold the Gibson to record producer and songwriter Chips Moman, who used it on hundreds of sessions in the 1960s and 1970s. It can be heard on Aretha Franklin's "Do Right Woman", for instance, and Wilson Pickett's "Mustang Sally". In the hands of session ace Reggie Young, it also played its part on the Moman-produced "Suspicious Minds", one of Elvis's most exciting records, which was recorded at Moman's Memphis studio in 1969.

With that kind of pedigree behind it, it's not surprising that the Super 400C attracted great interest when it came up for auction in Christie's, London, in April 2000. It was eventually sold for £67,550 (over $100,000).

The guitar that every budding rock'n'roller wanted to own in the late 1950s was the Gibson ES-350, for the simple reason that it was the one used by Chuck Berry on his landmark series of singles for the American R&B label Chess Records – and in every publicity picture too. An instrument in excellent condition could sell for as much as £15,000 ($22,500) today. Even more valuable is the

ES-335, which emerged around 1958, and is regarded as the king of Gibson's thinline archtop electric models, perfect for blues playing. It was also the favourite of guitar aces such as Britain's premier rock'n'roll picker, Joe Brown. A reissue edition from 1982, the ES-335 Dot, can itself sell for several thousand pounds.

The third of the premier rock guitar brands is Gretsch – who were scarcely represented in the Clapton sale, because he never found their models to his particular taste. Indeed, some guitar aficionados have complained that despite their obvious class, Gretsch instruments are renowned more for their superb appearance than their sound or durability. But there is no doubt that the single cutaway models made by the company between 1954 and 1961, many of which were endorsed by Nashville country guitar ace Chet Atkins, will never go out of style. They were popular with rockabilly guitar heroes such as Carl Perkins, which was enough in itself to make the Gretsch the guitar of choice for George Harrison, as soon as the Beatles had earned enough money for him to afford one. He picked up his first Duo Jet model in the summer of 1961, added a Country Gentleman two years later, and then treated himself to a Tennessean at the end of 1963. Another famous Gibson to have appeared at auction was Hank Williams' early 1950s Southern Jumbo acoustic. Gibson designed this guitar as a tribute to the South, and launched it in 1942. An eager fan paid $112,500 (£79,000) for the privilege of owning it.

The Chet Atkins Tennessean and Chet Atkins Country Gentleman models remain firm favourites from the mid-1950s, while many collectors also yearn for other Gretsch instruments from the same period, such as the White Penguin, the White Falcon, the Rancher and the Roundup. Gretsch was almost always linked with country music and rockabilly, however, and so its guitars failed to appeal so much to the mostly blues-oriented musicians who pioneered the 1960s rock movement. But the appeal of Gretsch guitars was undoubtedly enhanced by the endorsement of the Beatles.

One of the most distinctive sounds of the 1960s was the "jingle-jangle" twelve-string of the Rickenbacker 360-12. This was introduced in 1964, and one of the first famous musicians to own a copy was George Harrison, who obtained it during the group's first US visit that February and was seen using it in the Beatles' first movie, *A Hard Day's Night*. That in turn inspired Jim (later known as Roger) McGuinn of the Byrds to track one down, and his Rickenbacker riffs became central to the group's early success. Dozens of groups and hundreds of guitarists have subsequently mimicked McGuinn's style, and the 360-12 has become *de rigueur* for anyone attempting to maintain the Byrds' tradition.

That wasn't the only contribution made to Beatles history by Rickenbacker guitars, though. John Lennon purchased his first Rickenbacker 325 model in Hamburg in 1960, and that instrument is still owned by his widow, Yoko Ono. George Harrison upgraded to a Rickenbacker 425 when he visited his sister in the USA late in 1963; and you can see that guitar in the museum at the Rock & Roll Hall Of Fame in Cleveland. Paul McCartney wasn't to be left out, as he acquired a Rickenbacker 4001S bass during the mid-1960s.

There are many more collectible guitars from the 1950s and 1960s, of course, from the Epiphone Casino (sought after because the Beatles used them, and John Lennon had his painted in psychedelic colours, rather than

*opposite: The Beatles helped to popularize Rickenbacker guitars around the world. George Harrison played this model, which was sold for £56,500 ($90,400) in 1999.*

for any sonic qualities) to the deliciously nostalgic sound of the electric sitar manufactured in the late 1960s by the Coral company, and heard on dozens of hit records over the next few years. Eric Clapton endorsed Guild guitars for many years; the early Rolling Stones and the Yardbirds both opted for the Harmony Stratotone; Paul McCartney famously used the Hofner Violin Bass from 1961 onwards, having already taken over early Beatle Stuart Sutcliffe's Hofner 333 bass in the early 1960s; and Silvertone and Danelectro also produced some intriguing instruments.

Into this last category comes the double-neck 3923 model manufactured by Danelectro between 1959 and 1969, which combined six-string electric and four-string electric bass instruments. Equally outlandish was the legendary Gibson Flying V, loved as much for its instantly recognizable "V" shape as for its sound. In the same year that they debuted that model (1958), Gibson also introduced the futuristic-looking Explorer, making just nineteen copies that year, three in 1959, and only a handful after that. A similarly bizarre shape was the trademark of the Gibson Firebird, introduced in 1963, which also boasted a raised centre section hosting the fretboard.

Moving back into the pre-rock era, aficionados of all musical tastes relish the acoustic sound of a Martin guitar. The company was launched way back in the 1840s, and virtually every instrument they made for the next 125 years has become a collector's item. Few, however, can ever hope to rival the $173,000 (around £108,000) raised by Clapton's 1974 Martin 000-28 at the Crossroads sale. Its closest contender was the D-18 from 1942, sold by Christie's in 1993 for £99,000 ($148,000). As you might expect, this instrument had some pedigree of its own: it was used by Elvis Presley on all five of his legendary Sun Records singles in 1954 and 1955.

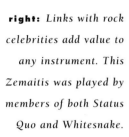

**right:** *Links with rock celebrities add value to any instrument. This Zemaitis was played by members of both Status Quo and Whitesnake.*

The hand-made instruments that came from the workshop of the American craftsman John D'Angelico between 1932 and his death in 1964 are also discussed in hushed tones by guitar-lovers. Then there is the visually unmistakeable National Duolian – certain of its place in the history books via many memorable folk, blues and country records, and immortalized in the words of Paul Simon's song "Graceland": "The Mississippi Delta was shining like a National guitar".

In unusual circumstances, guitars that have nothing of the elegance or reputation of the National Duolian can attract vast sums at auction. As every Beatles biography since the 1960s has noted, John Lennon's first guitar was bought for him by his Aunt Mimi – who passed into legend as the author of the famous quote, "The guitar's alright for a hobby, John, but you'll never make a living by it." In the mid-1950s, she purchased her nephew a Gallotone Champion acoustic guitar, which bore the legend: "Guaranteed Not To Split". That was no idle boast, as the instrument was sold at auction in 1999. Mimi had apparently had it restored shortly before Lennon's death, with the intention of giving it to him when he toured Britain in 1981. She even had a plaque mounted on it, bearing the words: "Remember you'll never earn your living by it". But after his murder, she couldn't bear to keep it in the house, and so she gave it to a Liverpool charity for disabled children. No guitar collector would give such an unprepossessing model house-room – except for the role it played in the early career of arguably Britain's most important rock musician. It was the guitar that Lennon was playing on the day when he met Paul McCartney, and on which McCartney effectively auditioned to join the pre-Beatles band, the Quarry Men. In the end, it changed hands for £155,500, almost a quarter of a million dollars.

That price was overshadowed in 2002, however, when two guitars owned by Jerry Garcia, the late fulcrum of the psychedelic band the Grateful Dead, were sold in New York. The two custom-made Alembic models, nicknamed "Tiger" and "Wolf" by Garcia, sold for $850,000 (£566,500) and $700,000 (£466,500) respectively – record auction prices for any rock and pop guitars.

Signed guitars are a staple of every rock auction, although the usual hierarchy applies: instruments signed by the Rolling Stones will outsell those bearing the autographs of the Who, who in turn outclass Status Quo or ZZ Top, and so on down the line. Almost all of these instruments were signed and originally sold for charity, and the value of the guitar itself is usually minimal on these occasions. As with publicity photographs or album sleeves, it's the signatures that provide most of the attraction.

Guitars have tended to dominate the instrument sections of pop and rock memorabilia auctions over the last two decades. But other instruments haven't been entirely overlooked. The piano on which John Lennon is said to have composed his classic song "Imagine" fetched an incredible £1.5 million ($2.25 million) at auction – leading collectors to speculate how much the more famous white piano that is seen in the video for Lennon's song might be worth.

**left:** *Beatles producer George Martin used this Bechstein piano to arrange the scores for hits by Elton John and Paul McCartney.*

# ICONIC JAZZ INSTRUMENTS

Few musicians in the history of popular music have linked themselves so closely with the sound of a particular instrument as the trumpet maestro and jazz genius Miles Davis. Hence the excitement when a trumpet he used regularly at the height of his jazz-rock experiments in the late 1960s and early 1970s came up for sale in New York in 2000. Perhaps more importantly for some jazz aficionados, Dizzy Gillespie's Martin Committee trumpet, with its famous bent bell, appeared at auction at Christie's, New York, and realized in excess of $55,000 (£37,000).

The most significant collection of jazz-related material, however, was the Chan Parker Collection – a wide-ranging and eclectic set of personal and musical memorabilia that came under the hammer at Christie's, New York, in 1994. Chan was the widow of saxophonist Charlie "Bird" Parker who, like Miles Davis and Dizzy Gillespie, was one of the most influential musicians in jazz history. "Bird" was arguably the most vital pioneer of "be-bop", a free-flowing, turbulent strand of jazz that emerged in the 1940s and carried all before it for the next few decades. By helping to break down orthodox song structures, Parker effectively invented the music that we recognize as "jazz" today.

His widow's collection ran to some eighty-three lots, which included many fascinating music manuscripts, letters, contracts, and even Bird's income tax returns and driver's licence. There were awards he had been given by the leading US jazz magazine, *Down Beat*, and all sorts of other personal ephemera. But the star lot was a Grafton alto sax, made out of white plastic. Parker had been given the instrument by an Englishman in 1950, and because it was so unusual and distinctive, it was easy to trace the occasions on which he played it in public. Although it was a "cheap" saxophone of no intrinsic musical or financial value, Parker's Grafton fetched an incredible $135,000 (£90,000) by virtue of its association with an all-time jazz legend.

Despite its reputation amongst music critics as America's most significant contribution to twentieth-century music, jazz has as yet made relatively little impression on the world's auction rooms – with the notable exception of the Chan Parker sale. Yet it is quite possible that instruments and other artefacts linked to the jazz "greats" will come into their own long after some of the more ephemeral rock and pop figures of recent years have faded from the memory.

BOB REISNER Presents

"BIRD"
CHARLIE PARKER
AND HIS ALL STARS

DREW MOORE — Tenor          WALTER BISHOP JR. — Piano
ART MARGAN — Drums          TED KOTICH — Bass

Sunday, June 6
9:30 P.M. to 2 A.M.

OPEN DOOR
55 WEST 3rd STREET

jazz at massey hall
volume three | quintet

*chapter four*

# COSTUMES AND PERSONAL EFFECTS

**left:** *These snakeskin boots were once owned by Brian Jones of the Rolling Stones.*

What gives rock its power to capture the hearts and minds of generation after generation? It's the combination of music, attitude and image – and two of those qualities often combine to create stage costumes that evoke all the mystery and menace of star performers.

Even in the days before video clips became the main vehicle for transporting new rock music to the masses, a well-designed, visually striking costume was guaranteed to win its wearer at least a moment of the public's attention. In a handful of cases, the clothes have become synonymous with the artists who wore them.

**right:** *One of the trademark collarless stage suits worn by the Beatles in 1963.*

A gold lamé suit automatically brings back memories of Elvis Presley. Even though he rarely wore such garb on stage, its appearance on one album cover was enough to give it icon status. Likewise the range of jumpsuits he wore during his final years in Las Vegas are forever associated with "the King". Collarless Pierre Cardin suits instantly evoke the halcyon days of Beatlemania. Imagine a black basque, and it's hard not to envisage Madonna on stage. Outrageous glasses and foot-high platform shoes? It must be Elton John.

Some artists discover the perfect visual foil for their music, and keep it for an entire career. Others insist on a different look for each era, or even each album. Certain costumes – such as David Bowie's *Ziggy Stardust* garb, or the suits the Beatles wore on the cover of *Sgt. Pepper's Lonely Hearts Club Band* – have become enshrined in history.

There are only four *Sgt. Pepper* suits in existence, and all of them still remain in the keeping of the individual Beatles' families. It's difficult to imagine any circumstances (beyond perhaps a charity auction) in which, say, Paul McCartney's *Pepper* suit might ever come up for auction. Even in the extremely unlikely event that it was stolen, it would be impossible to sell, because its origin and rightful owner would be obvious to any potential purchaser.

So the *Pepper* suit has to remain a dream, for even the most wealthy of collectors. But over the past twenty years, a number of exotic and attractive pieces of stage clothing with superstar connections have come up for sale at pop and rock memorabilia auctions.

Exactly the same questions of authenticity come into play here as with instruments and other items once owned by the stars. Ideally, the seller will be able to provide visual evidence that the costume was used on stage, in the shape of photographs or film clips. The vendor will also be required to provide some form of legal declaration supporting the provenance of the item – even if the person who is selling the clothing is a relative or close friend of the star in question.

**left:** *This stage suit, worn by Buddy Holly on his 1957 US tour with the Crickets, fetched £10,575 ($14,800) at auction in 2001.*

On very rare occasions, however, the authenticity of stage costumes is absolutely beyond question. Such was the case when Elton John auctioned a large proportion of his collection of his own ephemera and stagewear. A major part of that 1988 sale was devoted to artefacts he had used or worn on stage, several of which have since reappeared at other auctions.

An inveterate accumulator in his own right (he later sold one of the most impressive record collections ever assembled publicly), Elton John made the decision to part company with large portions of his wardrobe, furniture, jewellery and other possessions when, in his own words, "My house became knee-deep in everything. I want to build a home rather than a museum. Dispose of the lot. No going halfway!" The sale featured not just stage costumes but many of his trademark spectacles – the most outlandish of which sold for no less than £3,500 ($6,000). More recently, the musician has staged a series of further sales of his personal effects and clothing, designed to raise funds for charities supporting victims of AIDS.

One of Elton John's superstar associates has also staged a sale of costumes and clothing, although on a rather more local scale. Back in 1982, Eric Clapton donated many

*right: Appropriately enough, this cream suit was worn by Eric Clapton on the cover of the Cream album* Goodbye *in 1969.*

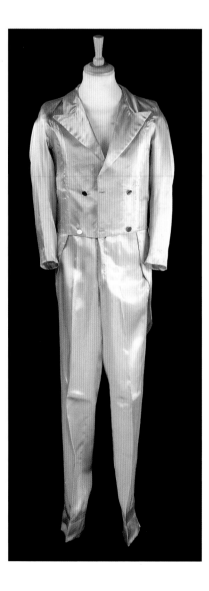

items from his wardrobe to a charity sale in the village hall of Cranleigh in Surrey, England, where he lived at the time. One of the visitors to the sale took the opportunity to ask Clapton if the blue denim jacket he'd worn at George Harrison's Concert For Bangla Desh in 1971 was up for sale, and was pointed in the right direction by the guitarist himself. Nearly twenty years later, that jacket was offered for sale at a Christie's auction in London, and fetched £2,585 ($3,800).

The same London sale also featured a Clapton stage suit that had been seen all over the world. The silver sateen jacket and trousers were worn by the musician for the photo session that produced the cover artwork for Cream's last album, *Goodbye*. With suitable authentication, it went under the hammer for £12,925 ($19,000).

A similar but rather less lavish stage suit, described as having an "ivory linen effect", formed part of an extensive sale in New York of Buddy Holly artefacts. In 2001, ten years after it was first sold, the suit – worn by Holly during a US tour with the Crickets in 1957, two years before his death – resurfaced in London and fetched £10,575 ($15,000).

During his prolific film career, between 1956 and 1969, Elvis Presley obviously wore a vast

**left:** *Elton John bought this pierrot costume in the 1970s, and wore it in his 1981 promotional video "Chloe".*

**right:** *Although Elvis Presley has become synonymous with the jumpsuit, he also wore this two-piece suit on stage in the 1970s.*

**left:** *Elvis wore this floral shirt in his 1970 film* That's The Way It Is, *as the edition of* Elvis Monthly *magazine below confirms.*

ALWAYS 100% ELVIS

26th Year
$2

Elvis MONTHLY

No 310

95p

**right:** Madonna's exotic stage costumes have attracted great interest at auction. This black bustier sold for £9,250 ($13,000).

selection of costumes – relatively few of which have ever cropped up at auction. In 2001, however, a sale in New York provided collectors with the chance to buy the beige blazer he wore in the 1962 movie *Girls! Girls! Girls!*, and the yellow linen jacket he sported as the leading man in 1966's *Spin Out*. However, most in demand seem to be the flamboyant stage costumes from the Las Vegas years. In the late 1990s, the Graceland archive held a mammoth sale of Elvis material. Amongst the collection was an elaborate stage cape richly encrusted with an American eagle (so heavily decorated that it would prove too heavy for Elvis to wear, a shorter one being made), which, even though used only once, sold for $105,250 (£75,000).

When it comes to stagewear, however, little in pop history has ever left such a mark upon the memory (or, at least, the male memory) as the trademark basques worn by Madonna during her "Blonde Ambition" tour.

Equally intimate and famous was the Jean Paul Gaultier stage bra, made of black satin but with pink stitching to accentuate the conical cups that Madonna also sported during that tour. One such item was offered to the winner of a BBC Radio 1 phone-in competition in 1990. Rather embarrassingly for the Corporation, the disc jockey who was running the quiz made a mistake and awarded the prize to someone who gave an incorrect answer. To prevent a prolonged argument, the BBC had to persuade Madonna's management to donate a second bra, so that the rightful winner could also be rewarded. The reward was partly financial, as one of those bras sold at a London auction in 2001 for £14,100 (nearly $20,000).

**right:** *David Bowie occasionally wore this jacket during his "Ziggy Stardust" concerts in 1973.*

Madonna is far from being the only artist whose visual presence has become synonymous with a particular look or costume. The American rock band Kiss emerged in the mid-1970s with a flamboyant image totally at odds with the rather serious and staid atmosphere of the time. For more than a decade, they were never glimpsed in public without their "mask" make-up, and their stage clothes were equally outlandish. Amongst the unusual items that have surfaced at auction recently have been a pair of platform boots worn by Kiss bass guitarist Gene Simmons that epitomize their glam-rock appeal.

*below: A pair of custom-made pink leather platform shoes that were made for Gene Simmons c.1974.*

More surreal still was the rhinestone glove affected both on and off stage by Michael Jackson. One example sold for £16,500 ($28,000) at a sale in 1991, but despite its unique nature, its value may well have slipped since then, as Jackson's reputation has been damaged by a barrage of bad publicity since the mid-1990s.

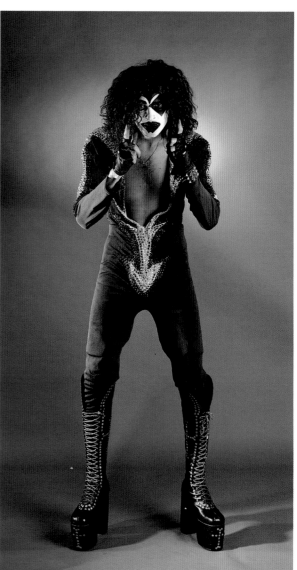

*right: One of four spectacular costumes made for and worn by the members of Kiss in their first film, Kiss Meets The Phantom, 1978. All four were sold together in 1993 for £20,900 ($31,500).*

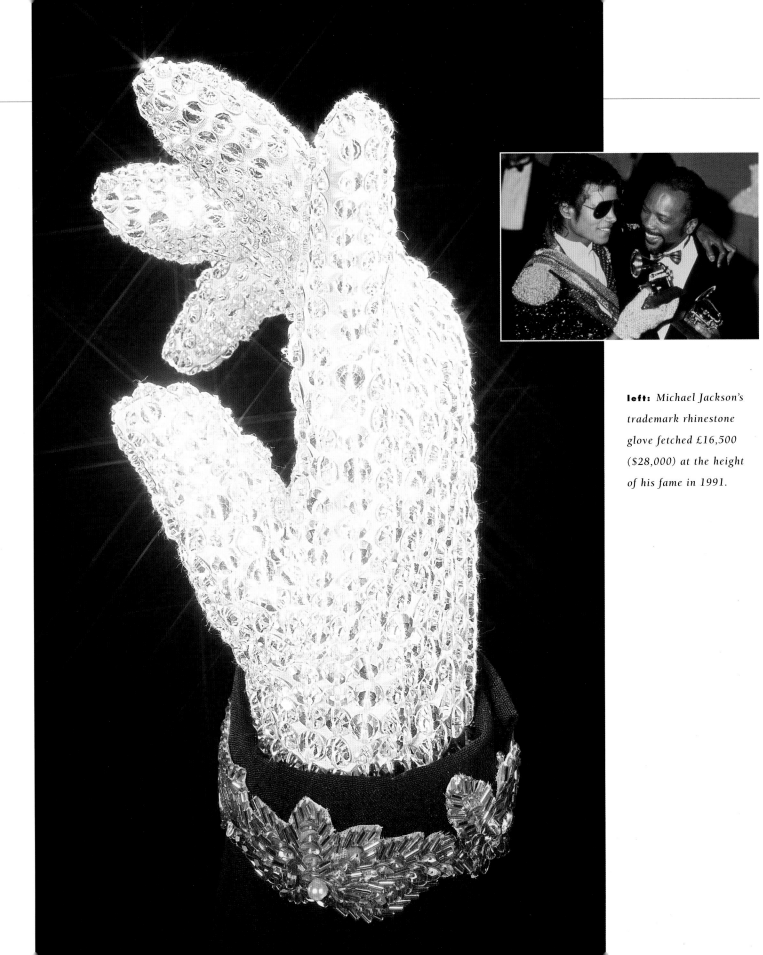

**left:** *Michael Jackson's trademark rhinestone glove fetched £16,500 ($28,000) at the height of his fame in 1991.*

## PERSONAL EFFECTS

Stage costumes have a tangible link with a pop star's career and fame. But many more personal effects connected with rock stars – almost always those stars who have met tragically early deaths – have also come up for sale over the years. Not all collectors prefer to travel down this road: someone who might pay several thousand dollars for a suit worn by Elvis on stage might not be so intrigued or inspired by a piece of furniture from Presley's home. Others relish the opportunity to own something that was part of the star's daily life, even if the object in itself has little star quality.

Two of the most fascinating collections of personal effects both took place in 1991. In New York, the Buddy Holly estate auctioned a vast array of items linked with the 1950s rock'n'roller. It was then thirty-two years since Holly had died in a fateful air crash, and bidders competed for items as diverse as his birth certificate, his diploma from Lubbock Senior High School, a pair of his glasses and a high school ring.

Two months later in London, John Lennon's first wife, Cynthia, took the brave but briefly controversial decision to auction many items from the home she had shared with John in the 1960s. The Cynthia Lennon Collection included such unlikely pieces of pop memorabilia as a mahogany writing table, a pair of Persian rugs, an ivory chess set from India and a cocktail cabinet in the shape of a globe; but Lennon collectors snapped them all up.

Also featured in the sale were more obviously collectible items, such as an Ivor Novello Award Lennon had been given for his part in writing "She Loves You", a large collection of drawings in his hand on Apple Corps paper, and an almost unbearably poignant letter from husband to wife in which Lennon bemoaned his own shortcomings as a father. In their very different ways, all these items cast a little more light on the Lennon enigma.

Some personal effects have a less immediate connection with the star in question. Elvis Presley was famed for his generosity, with both friends and strangers. It was quite common for him to make a quick phone call and order a new car or gold jewellery for everyone who happened to be in the room at the time – one of the reasons his estate was worth so little when he died in 1977. So it's not surprising that an array of former Presley associates have been able to offer gifts from "the King" for sale.

In 2001, a more typical sign of Presley's friendship emerged, as a fourteen-carat gold ring was offered at auction in New York. Adding to its value was the fact that it was encrusted with fourteen single-cut diamonds. Of course, it certainly didn't hurt in financial terms when it could be proved that Presley had worn this ring during his wedding ceremony with Priscilla Beaulieu in 1967.

An unusual item was featured in the catalogue for the Buddy Holly sale held in 1991, reappearing at a New York auction in December 2000. This was the high school ticket book used by Charles Holley (note the original

*below: An opal ring from the late 1960s, once worn by Jimi Hendrix, and authenticated by one of his girlfriends.*

spelling!) in 1952, four years before he changed his name and enjoyed three brief years in the limelight.

Much more macabre was the wristwatch that Holly was wearing on the night in February 1959 when he, the Big Bopper, Ritchie Valens and the pilot died. They were killed when the light plane hired to take them to their next concert venue crashed during a blizzard. On the reverse of the watch was etched the message "Buddy Holly 12-1-58", showing that he had had it in his possession for just two months and two days before he was killed. Morbid? Maybe. But similar items relating to historical figures are now centrepieces in museums around the world, and it's quite possible that in another 100 years, Buddy Holly's watch will be on display in a cabinet alongside the timepiece carried by Abraham Lincoln when he was assassinated.

**left:** *Two pairs of cufflinks and tie tac, rare personal mementos from the Estate of Buddy Holly that sold for £552 ($880) in 1997.*

# FAMOUS AUTOMOBILES

For the collector with a garage as deep as their wallet, the ultimate piece of personal memorabilia must be a car. Not altogether surprisingly, the rock star with the largest collection of automobiles proved to be Elton John, who auctioned twenty post-war classics at a special sale in the summer of 2001. His Rolls-Royce Phantom VI limousine fetched £223,750 ($320,000); the entire sale raised £1.9 million, nearly $2.75 million.

Elton John's car was far from being the first rock vehicle to reach the auction room, however. A 1970 Mercedes Benz 600 Pullman that had been owned and used by John Lennon in the late 1960s and early 1970s sold for £137,500 (almost $200,000) in London in 1989; fortunately, its value wasn't affected when it was clamped by an over-zealous traffic warden while it was on display before the sale! A decade later, a 1956 Lincoln Continental Mk II previously owned by Elvis Presley sold for $295,000 (£205,000) in – appropriately enough for "the King" – Las Vegas, where he played more concerts than in any other city in America.

There is absolutely no competition for the status of the most valuable rock star car ever sold, however. During the late 1960s, John Lennon frequently amazed his fellow road users when he cruised past them in his psychedelic Rolls-Royce limousine – specially painted for him by the members of the Fool art-and-music group. In 1986, this perfect encapsulation of the spirit of the 1960s went under the hammer – for no less than $2.3 million, or £1.6 million.

When U2 were promoting their *Achtung Baby* album, they acquired a Trabant car, one of the no-frills, utterly basic saloons that were virtually the only vehicles to be found on the streets of Eastern Europe before the fall of the Berlin Wall. This unlikely collectible was then spray-painted and signed (in paint, of course) by U2's collaborator and producer, Brian Eno. Its value as a vehicle was less than zero, except in kitsch terms, and the Trabant should perhaps be classed alongside promotional gimmicks like press packs and desk calendars rather than with the lavish limousines once owned by Elton John. But regardless of its status, it still sold for £1,150 (over $1,600) – making it probably the most valuable Trabant car anywhere in the world!

1 and 2: *A sample of Elton John's automobile collection.*
3: *The Trabant used by U2 to promote their album* Achtung Baby.

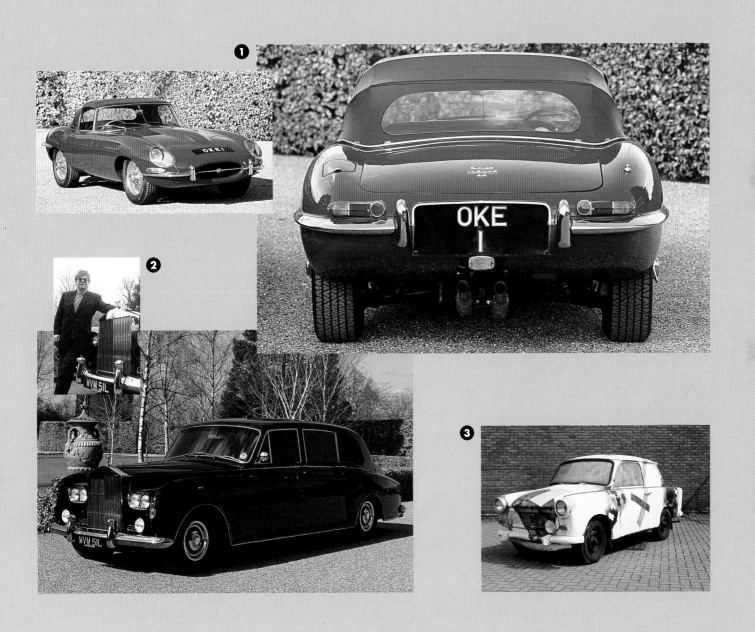

*chapter five*

The Oxford Dictionary offers two definitions of the word "poster". The first is "a large printed picture used for decoration"; the second: "a large printed picture, notice or advertisement, displayed in a public place".

Those two linked but crucially different definitions illustrate a key distinction that needs to be understood by anyone who wants to collect posters. Another way of approaching the same subject is to ask a question: what exactly are posters for?

On the surface, the answer seems simple. Posters are designed to advertise an event, a person or a company. They alert the outside world to the fact that a new record or movie is about to be released, that a concert is about to be staged, or that a particular artist or business concern is still plying their trade, whatever that might be.

Almost all of the most collectible pop and rock posters fall into that category. Whether they were stating factual information in the most prosaic way imaginable, like many 1950s and 1960s concert posters, or conjuring up an exotic world of the imagination, like the psychedelic posters that came out of California in the late 1960s, their primary function was to tell the public what was happening.

At some point in the mid-1960s, however, the function of the poster began to widen. As cheap colour printing became more widespread, it was possible for publishers, publicists and promoters to mass-produce posters that, in the past, had to be printed in much smaller and more expensive runs. The pop industry seized on this innovation and began to offer consumers the chance to buy poster portraits of their favourite stars. Magazines and newspapers often included free pull-out posters for their readers. By the late 1960s,

**right:** *A valuable poster for a concert showcasing a unique array of jazz talent, at New York's prestigious Carnegie Hall in 1952.*

posters were often being offered as part of the packaging for new album releases. Record shops regularly carried posters amongst their stock; and by the early 1970s, they were as common as mass-produced "ten-by-eight" (25.4 x 20.3cm) glossy pop photos had been a decade earlier.

At the same time, the promoters and artists who created the psychedelic posters that swept across America and Britain from the mid-1960s realized that their artefacts were becoming instant collector's items, amongst people who treasured them as *objets d'art* in their own right, not just as a way of communicating information. Aficionados were ripping down the most attractive and

**left:** *This 1967 Jimi Hendrix poster was designed by the British psychedelic group Hapshash & The Coloured Coat.*

interesting concert posters as soon as they appeared on walls, or else begging spare copies from the promoters' staff. To meet this demand, longer runs of these posters were printed and sold, often long after the concerts they were advertising had taken place. The role of the poster had changed forever, complicating the market for collectors just at the time it was undergoing a dramatic expansion.

In recent years, posters have become a mini industry within the world of popular entertainment auctions. Christie's regularly stages auctions of film posters on both sides of the Atlantic, while all pop and rock sales routinely feature original items from the 1950s, 1960s and 1970s. As the market continues to grow, so does the sophistication of collectors' knowledge. The publication in 1987 of Paul Grushin's mammoth book *The Art Of Rock* introduced a much larger audience to the complexities and delights of the poster market. Since then, specialist titles such as Eric King's *A Collector's Guide To The Numbered Dance Posters Created For Bill Graham & The Family Dog: 1967–1973* and Fred Williams' *Rock Poster Price Guide* (both privately published in the USA) have given hardcore collectors an incredible level of information about different editions of posters and their respective values.

However, it's not necessary to be able to identify all the minute differences between four editions of a Bill Graham (who ran the legendary Fillmore venues in San Francisco and New York) psychedelic poster from 1968 to begin collecting in this field. The basic principles of collecting posters apply to all the different

**left:** *A publicity poster for Led Zeppelin's concert dates at the Empire Pool in Wembley, in London, during the early 1970s.*

specialist areas, and in many ways they simply reflect the same rules of collectability that we have discovered throughout this book. Very few posters printed after the punk explosion of the late 1970s have proved valuable or sought after enough to justify a place in a prominent rock and pop auction. The only exceptions to this general rule have been those that have been signed by major artists, such as Madonna, Paul McCartney or the Rolling Stones, and in those cases it is the signature that attracts buyers, rather than the poster itself.

The same hierarchy of artists that applies throughout the pop and rock field is equally valid in the field of posters. A Beatles concert poster from 1963 may have a much less attractive design than, say, a poster for Cliff Richard from the same year, but it will always fetch a higher price at auction. The picture may be slightly more complicated with psychedelic posters, where the identity of the graphic artist carries nearly as much weight as the star being promoted; but it's probably not a coincidence that the most highly priced psychedelic posters are usually those featuring Jimi Hendrix, the Grateful Dead, the Doors or Jefferson Airplane, rather than the lesser known Oxford Circle or Youngbloods.

In the case of concert posters from the 1950s and the first half of the 1960s, there is one crucial and simple way of distinguishing original artefacts from later reproductions. Before around 1965, posters were always printed on matt paper, in a set and standard size; afterwards they almost always appeared on glossy paper, and could be reproduced en masse in a bewildering variety of shapes and sizes.

**right:** *A typical poster from a 1960s UK package tour, featuring several hit acts and some relative unknowns.*

If you find a glossy poster advertising a concert from 1956 or 1963, it doesn't mean that the vendor is attempting to deceive the purchaser. As the copyright in early poster designs is often very difficult to establish, many manufacturers have mass-produced copies of vintage posters without pretending that they are selling originals. Common sense will usually make it clear that the pristine-looking and entirely undamaged poster for a 1956 Elvis Presley concert, on offer at a street market, is not a valuable collector's item, but simply a cheap and nostalgic souvenir.

Although it is not impossible for a vintage 1950s or 1960s poster to have survived the passing decades in immaculate condition, there will almost certainly be some telltale signs of ageing – scuffs, yellowing of paper, small tears and the like. Price alone can tell the story: if a dealer in a street market or a backstreet store is selling a 1960s concert poster for the same price as a modern item, then you're pretty safe to assume that it won't be an original. There are still bargains to be found, but anyone who sells posters for a living will know that vintage posters command serious prices these days.

Artefacts from the 1950s and 1960s have a built-in nostalgic factor that even the most loving facsimile can't match. That is one reason why so few serious collectors are interested in material originating in more recent years. Another is that the pop and rock collecting market began to develop in a big way around that period, and so aficionados were consciously preserving material with the collecting mentality in mind. In the 1960s and 1970s, posters might have been displayed on the bedroom wall; by the 1980s, potential collectors were carefully storing their finds out of direct sunlight and often entirely out of view. Far more posters from this period were saved for posterity, and as a result their values have remained much lower than for their vintage predecessors.

One other factor needs to be remembered when you're pricing your collection, or attempting to add to it. In general, collectors tend to be most attracted by artefacts from their own country. American aficionados generally prefer psychedelic posters from California and New York to those from Britain and Europe, and vice versa. That doesn't mean there is no market for transatlantic dealing, as many early UK Beatles posters find a home elsewhere in the world, while the same can be said of many choice psychedelic posters from San Francisco.

## VINTAGE POP POSTERS

Before 1966, even the biggest pop stars in the world performed on package tours featuring a variety of other artists, famous and otherwise, and their colleagues on tour weren't even necessarily other musical acts. After a couple of years touring the American South with fellow country musicians, Elvis Presley graduated to the big time in 1956 – whereupon his manager, Colonel Tom Parker, took the decision to make sure that his boy could never be outclassed by anyone else on the bill. As a result, fans who witnessed Elvis in concert between 1956 and 1958 usually had to endure a line-up of lame comedians and

**below:** *A souvenir poster by 1960s psychedelic artists Hapshash & the Coloured Coat, c. 1967; this poster is purely decorative, rather than one produced for a concert.*

**left:** *The short-lived psychedelic group Dantalian's Chariot were the focal point of this highly sought-after poster from 1968.*

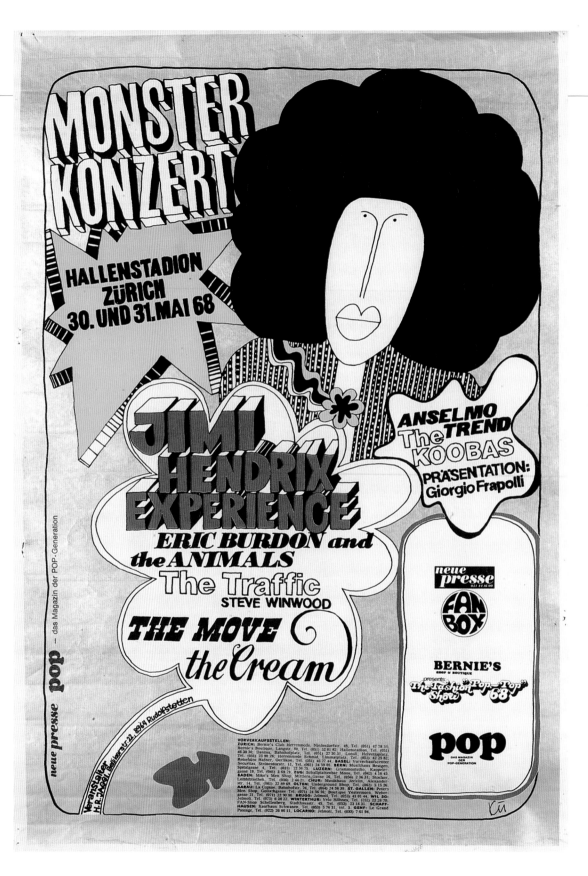

**right:** *Jimi Hendrix posters
remain the most sought-after
examples of psychedelic art. This
Swiss design dates from May 1968.*

novelty acts, none of whom represented the slightest threat to his supremacy on stage.

The early history of the Beatles can be traced through concert posters, as they rose through the ranks of Liverpool's rock'n'roll and beat musicians, before becoming national and then international stars. At the start of the 1960s, their name was often included amongst many other Merseybeat bands of similar stature, such as Gerry & the Pacemakers and Rory Storm & the Hurricanes (Ringo Starr's outfit until he joined the Beatles in August 1962). By 1962, they were usually billed as headliners in Liverpool – unless an American star such as Little Richard was in town, in which case they were back amongst the support acts. Posters for the Little Richard Show at the Tower Ballroom in New Brighton and the Liverpool Empire, both showing the Beatles down the bill, have sold for £4,000–£5,000 ($6,000–$7,500).

By 1963, the Beatles were British pop stars in their own right, although early in that year they still weren't considered a strong enough attraction to top a national bill. A poster from the Birmingham Hippodrome in March 1963 shows that the top-of-the-bill acts were "America's Exciting Chris Montez" and "America's Fabulous Tommy Roe". Then followed a list of long-forgotten names, from "Glamorous Debbie Lee" to "Your 208 DJ Tony Marsh", before the poster mentioned "Britain's Dynamic Beatles – 'Love Me Do', 'Please Please Me'". At least the Beatles' pictures were on display, however, which is more than Tony Marsh or glamorous Debbie Lee achieved, and if a star makes a pictorial appearance on a poster, then that always makes it a more saleable item than an artefact that simply lists their name.

Elvis Presley, the Beatles, Jimi Hendrix and, to a slightly lesser extent, the Rolling Stones can transform a vintage pop poster from a £300 ($450) souvenir into a £3,000 ($4,500) collector's item. A little below them in the auction hierarchy come artists such as the Doors and Bob Dylan; a step further down, you'd find the Who, the Grateful Dead, the Kinks, Cream and the Yardbirds. With the exception of the Grateful Dead, who restricted most of their early appearances to California, and Bob Dylan, who as a supposed "folk" artist was allowed to appear without any supporting acts, all of those names can be found in the most incongruous of company on 1950s and 1960s package tour posters.

Most of those items were printed in a standard size measured in inches, thirty high by twenty across (76.2 x 50.8cm). But exactly the same artwork was usually available in one or two other forms. The posters themselves were supplied to the theatres by the concert promoters; unlike film posters, which were almost always sent pre-folded in envelopes, concert posters usually arrived in rolled form and were therefore uncreased.

Miniature versions of the poster designs would often be seen on display in the theatre, or in local shops, in the form of stiff window cards, measuring perhaps 38 x 25.4cm (15 x 10in). Smaller still were the handbills given out to people attending earlier concerts at the same venue.

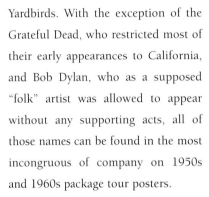

The vast majority of posters that were printed for package tours were slapped onto the wall of the theatre and nearby billboards. Some of those were carefully torn down by fans; on other occasions, admirers of a particular artist were able to beg or steal a poster from the promoter, or else retrieve an excess copy from the printer. Collecting for financial value only arrived with the birth of psychedelic poster art in California.

## PSYCHEDELIC POSTERS

The Oxford Dictionary definition of "psychedelic" is either "(of drugs) that make the user hallucinate"; or "having intensely vivid colours, sounds, etc. like those experienced while hallucinating".

In the first sense of the word, the psychedelic experience was provided by the hallucinogenic drug LSD, which swept through the counter-culture in America, Britain and Europe from the mid-1960s onwards. Under its dramatic influence, users claimed that they entered a world of limitless potential, where the entire universe was at their command, and all their senses were prey to extreme stimulation. The psychedelic "trip" could be good or bad; but most psychedelic music and art preferred to join the "vibe" of the era, and accentuate the positive.

In musical terms, the word "psychedelic" has been used to describe two linked but quite different sets of artists: British acts such as Pink Floyd, Soft Machine and (in 1967, at least) the Beatles and the Rolling Stones; and American "acid-rockers", such as the Grateful Dead, Jefferson Airplane and Quicksilver Messenger Service. The US bands channelled their LSD experience into lengthy, free-flowing improvisation; the British acid trip was expressed with more whimsical music and lyrical imagery, full of magic pixies and exotic landscapes.

These usually featured tear-off booking forms at the bottom, and were obviously designed to stimulate ticket sales. Window cards may also have featured space for fans to fill out an order for tickets. In both cases, these items are more valuable if these forms are still intact and have been left unfilled. But even without the forms, handbills are still sought after by many collectors.

alexis korner
alex harvey
creation
charlie brown's
clowns
champion jack
dupree
denny laine
gary farr
graham bond
ginger johnson
jacob's ladder
construction co.
move
one one seven
pink floyd
poetry band
purple gang
pretty things
pete townshend
poison bellows
soft.machine
sun trolley
social deviants
stalkers
the utterly incredible
too long ago
to remember
sometimes shouting
at people
marc sullivan
martin doughty
maureen pape
john pape
mike stocks
noel murphy
dave russell
christopher logue
barry fantoni
ron geeson
john fahey
mike horowitz
alex trocchi
mike kenshall
yoko ono
binder edwards
& vaughan
26 kingly street
the flies
robert ransell

international times
free speech benefit
alexandra palace N.22
8pm saturday
29 april » sun 30
tickets £1
in advance » only

indica better books colletts
dobells dave curtis 57 greek
st w.1 ger 1548 and main
it distributors
or your local agent
bus shuttle from wood green ⊖
highgate ⊖ 8:12pm

14 HOUR TECHNICOLOR DREAM

**left:** *The highly collectible poster for one of the seminal UK psychedelic events, held in London in spring 1967.*

When it came to poster art, the differences were less extreme. It was still quite easy to distinguish American examples from those produced elsewhere in the world, but almost all the psychedelic designers shared a taste for swirling, hypnotic imagery, as if one were staring into the abyss; bright, sometimes lurid clashes of colour; and visual elements plucked from vintage sources, such as nineteenth-century "wild west" paintings and Pre- Raphaelite nudes.

The overall effect was a sense of sensory and artistic liberation, reflecting the explorations of the infinite that were reported by those who experimented with LSD. The old-school style of direct communication was replaced by a much more oblique approach. In 1964, the average pop poster contained a simple list of names, dates and places, accompanied by a photo or two. Its 1967 equivalent often completely obscured the details of the concert that it was theoretically advertising. As the Canadian cultural guru Marshall McLuhan put it in a phrase much quoted at the time, "The medium is the message."

*opposite: A rare concert poster for the "First International Pop Festival", Rome.*

The earliest psychedelic posters emerged in America in 1965, advertising concerts by the San Francisco acid-rock pioneers the Charlatans, or (in the case of "Can You Pass The Acid Test?") early events at which participants were offered a baptism in LSD. In February 1966, the Fillmore theatre in San Francisco was staging its first shows by bands such as Jefferson Airplane, under the auspices of legendary promoter Bill Graham. He subsequently widened his empire to include the Winterland Ballroom in San Francisco and the Fillmore East in New York, eventually becoming America's leading rock promoter. Meanwhile, the Fillmore briefly also became the

location for a set of promoters called the Family Dog, whose mantle was quickly taken over by Chet Helms, the manager of Big Brother & the Holding Company (featuring Janis Joplin). He soon moved the Family Dog promotions to the Avalon Ballroom in San Francisco.

The Family Dog and Bill Graham Presents promotions provided the most memorable concerts – and poster art – of the West Coast acid-rock explosion. Artists Wes Wilson, Victor Moscoso, Rick Griffin, Alton Kelley and Stanley Mouse – collectively dubbed "The San Francisco Five" – created the best-loved and most enduring images, and Kelley and Mouse's names became indelibly linked in history when they opened a joint studio.

Collectors have adopted a standard system for numbering the concerts, and posters, from both the Family Dog and Bill Graham Presents. Most rock fans are at least dimly aware that US psychedelic posters from the period between 1966 and 1970 are collector's items. Yet prices can vary enormously, even for different examples of the same poster. There is also the complication of handbills and, in some cases, postcards that duplicate the artwork on the posters in miniature form.

As mentioned earlier, the first "edition" or "state" of these posters was prepared before the concerts; thereafter, copies were manufactured as pieces of art (and potential collectibles) in their own right. Both might have been printed in the same year, yet whereas the first edition of something like Wes Wilson's "The Quick & The Dead" (advertising a Quicksilver and Grateful Dead show from the Avalon in June 1966) might sell for as much as $2,000 (£1,400), the virtually identical second edition can be picked up for just $50 or £35. As the differences between the two editions can vary from one poster to the next, there is sadly no substitute for expertise (and the reference books mentioned on page 108) when it comes to telling the two apart.

Equally baffling to the newcomer is the fact that some Kelley & Mouse designs sell for several thousand dollars, while others, sometimes featuring exactly the same bands, raise only a fraction of that amount. Certain examples have become classics, however, such as Rick Griffin's "Flying Eyeball" (used to promote Jimi Hendrix concerts at both the Fillmore and Winterland in February 1968); "Zig Zag", a Kelley & Mouse design for Big Brother and Quicksilver at the Avalon in June 1966; and the unforgettable "Skull & Roses" by the same team, which was first used for the Avalon in September 1966, but ended up presenting the Grateful Dead with a visual signifier that survived for the rest of their career.

Britain's most famous rivals to Kelley & Mouse and Rick Griffin were Martin Sharp (actually from Australia) and Hapshash & the Coloured Coat (alias Nigel Waymouth and Michael English). Sharp's portraits of Bob Dylan ("Blowing In The Wind") and Jimi Hendrix ("Explosion") regularly turn up at auction, while he reached his largest audience by designing the cover of Cream's album *Disraeli Gears*. (That wasn't his only contribution to the record, as he also penned the lyrics for the song "Tales Of Brave Ulysses".)

Hapshash's equally memorable work formed part of the Osiris series, commissioned to promote gigs at the London underground club UFO. The first appeared in February 1967, the final one a little over a year later. In between, Hapshash produced highly collectible designs for Soft Machine, the Move, the Who and the Mothers Of Invention, besides launching a short-lived recording career in their own right.

In terms of publicity, perhaps the most prominent group of artists at work in London in the late 1960s were a Dutch team called the Fool, who also veered back and forth between design work and recording. Their highest profile came when they were adopted by the Beatles as in-house designers, customizing John Lennon's Rolls-Royce limousine with psychedelic paintwork, offering a design for the group's 1968 double-album that was ultimately rejected, and decorating the outside wall of the Beatles' Apple retail store in London's Baker Street.

Psychedelia only held sway in the rock mainstream for little more than a year, and by 1968 most of the original acid inspiration of 1966–67 had evaporated. The British rock movement veered into progressive (or "prog") rock; America divided its attention between hard rock, country rock and the burgeoning soft-rock sound of the singer-songwriters. Yet the visual style invented by the best psychedelic artists survived much longer, and in the case of the Grateful Dead, it became their trademark until their demise in 1995.

San Francisco and London were far from being the only centres of rock art in the late 1960s – original posters for legendary festivals such as Monterey and Woodstock are renowned collector's items, while art for concerts by the likes of Jimi Hendrix is collectible regardless of its geographical origin. Yet the British capital and the American West Coast remained the key centres of innovation during that turbulent period. A decade later, a radically different sound, and look, once again brought London back to the forefront of the world of poster art. After several years in which over-serious music and staid artwork had been the order of the day, a bohemian influence re-entered the rock scene.

*right: This 1976 poster for a key concert in the early history of punk rock fetched £3,525 ($5,288) at a 2000 sale, which was ten times its expected price.*

## PUNK POSTERS

During the 1970s, rock stars became increasingly distanced from their fans. The most successful groups of the era – the Rolling Stones, the Who, Led Zeppelin, the Eagles, Fleetwood Mac, Black Sabbath and many more – abandoned the relatively intimate live shows in clubs, theatres and cinemas that had been the hallmark of 1960s pop. This was the age of arena rock, when rock bands filled cavernous halls, or even stadiums, that had been built to host major sporting events. The days of lining after the show for an autograph were long gone; in the 1970s, fans

were lucky to be able to see their idols as anything more than inch-high figures in the extremely long distance.

Rock was now a global phenomenon, and as the corporations took hold, marketing became a higher priority than music. In the 1960s, artists had regularly released two or more albums a year, and several singles besides; increasingly, in the 1970s and beyond, major stars left several years between each release. Each new territory that was conquered by rock represented fresh ground to be exploited. Often the coast-to-coast series of concerts was replaced by the world tour, with each nation's fans being rewarded by just one or two mega-shows in baseball or football stadiums. Likewise the music itself was becoming equally overblown, often characterized by pretentious lyrics and long self-indulgent instrumental solos.

Many fans were happy to go with the flow; but there was an undercurrent of alienation and bitterness, affecting young record-buyers and musicians alike, that had to find an outlet. The result was punk – utterly basic, aggressive, anarchic, do-it-yourself rock that combined

**below:** *This poster for the Sex Pistols' third single is all the more collectible for having been signed by designer Jamie Reid.*

: NEW SINGLE ON VIRGIN RECORDS VS184 :

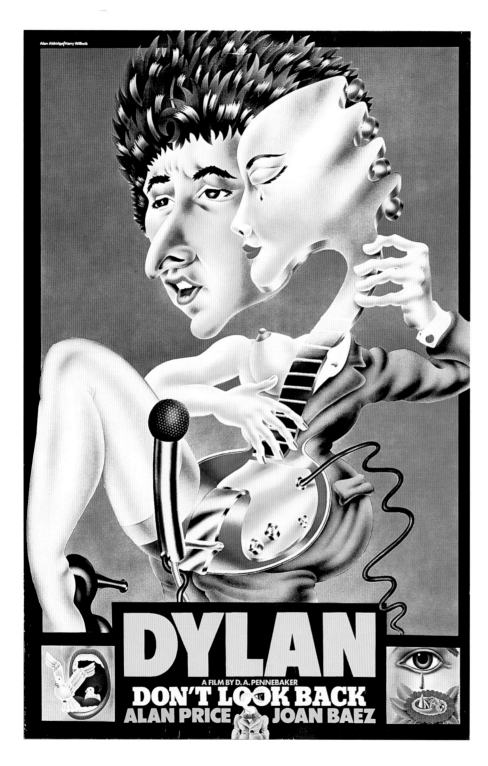

the immediacy of 1950s rock'n'roll with a cynicism and despair reflecting late 1970s society.

Punk hit Britain and America in markedly different ways. American punk was artier and more "adult"; British punk was musically more simple and direct. In Britain, the visual impact of punk, via posters for example, was hugely influenced by the work of one man, Jamie Reid, the visual genius behind the Sex Pistols. Almost single-handedly, Reid conceived and created in the late 1970s the graphic and pictorial identity of the Sex Pistols – and, as a result, the entire punk movement.

## FILM POSTERS

The degree of interest in collecting film posters has risen alongside the boom in the pop and rock memorabilia market in recent years. Not surprisingly, the two fields have often overlapped. Elvis Presley was the first rock star to make a regular impact on the big screen, and although critics are sceptical about the worth of all but a handful of his thirty-one movies (plus a couple of on-the-road documentaries), original US and UK posters from his earliest films like *Loving You* and *Jailhouse Rock* have sold for £1,000 ($1,500) or more.

Original posters for the Beatles' four feature films – *A Hard Day's Night*, *Help!*, the animated *Yellow Submarine* and the documentary *Let It Be* – are also consistently good sellers at auction. So is anything that is closely connected with individual members of the group, from *How I Won The War* (starring John Lennon) through *Candy* and *The Magic Christian* (both displaying Ringo Starr's acting talents) and *The Family Way* (with its Paul McCartney

**left:** *An original 1967 poster for* Don't Look Back, *one of the most memorable documentary films ever made.*

soundtrack) to *The Concert For Bangla Desh* (a charity endeavour staged by, and starring, George Harrison).

The Rolling Stones never made the movie they were always promising throughout the 1960s, but Mick Jagger did star in one of the great cult films of the period, *Performance*, one of a number of counter-culture pictures from the late 1960s and early 1970s that have proved to enjoy enduring popularity amongst successive generations of viewers, ensuring that their original posters will always be sought after. Other titles in a similar vein include *Easy Rider*, *Blow-Up* and *Two-Lane Blacktop* – none of them based around music, but all utilizing some element of rock's iconic power.

Other notable rock films from the era are also very popular amongst collectors of posters, including the festival movies *Woodstock* and *Monterey Pop*, the Bob Dylan documentary *Don't Look Back*, and "psychedelic" cash-ins such as *The Trip* and *Psych-Out*. Posters for films from the 1970s such as *The Man Who Fell To Earth* (starring David Bowie) and *The Great Rock'n'Roll Swindle* (a satirical account of the Sex Pistols' rise to infamy) also attract great interest.

In fact, virtually every pop-related film poster from the first two decades of rock'n'roll is of potential interest to collectors. Anyone who is tempted to venture too deeply into this area needs to do some additional research, however. While almost all pop and rock posters exist in only one size and shape, film companies regularly produced many different designs for each new release, depending on whether they were intended for display on billboards, outside cinemas or inside lobbies. Thus there may be as many as five or six equally valid "original" posters for a film – multiplied, of course, by the number of countries in which the movie was released.

**left:** *A piece of original artwork used on the poster for the 1976 David Bowie film,* The Man Who Fell To Earth.

**left:** *The poster for the film* Two-Lane Blacktop *(1971) is revered by movie aficionados and collectors of rock memorabilia.*

# THE ART OF JAMIE REID

The person who almost single-handedly provided British punk with its visual identity was artist Jamie Reid. A close associate of Sex Pistols' manager Malcolm McLaren and clothes designer Vivienne Westwood, he was in on what McLaren later termed, claiming inspiration from the European avant-garde Situationist movement, "The Great Rock'n'Roll Swindle".

Reid popularized the cut-up newspaper headlines that became the standard punk style of announcing information – as seen on the Sex Pistols' debut album, *Never Mind The Bollocks*. More importantly, he brought a level of political provocation to the marketing of the Pistols that suggested there was a much wider agenda to their fame than simply disturbing the music establishment.

Virtually any punk poster designed in the UK between 1976 and the end of that decade captures at least a little of the spirit of the age. But Reid's work – whether he was promoting a new release or merely subverting a global institution such as American Express – became the defining image of a movement that was to have an enormous impact on all rock music that followed in its wake. It is arguable that, in the long term, Reid's art may prove to have left a more lasting impact on the music business than punk itself.

Although interest from collectors outside Britain has been slower to rise, London auction rooms regularly sell examples of his work. His most striking images – like the tarnished portrait of Her Majesty with a safety pin through her lip that he used to promote the Sex Pistols' "God Save The Queen" single – are eagerly sought after, whether they appear on handbills, stickers or more conventional rock posters. As with psychedelic posters, however, many of his designs have been republished over the years, especially when the Pistols briefly reformed for a tour in 1996. Pristine originals can easily fetch £1,000 ($1,500) plus, however, while his scarcest designs – such as the "Sid Vicious Olympia De Paris" poster produced for the Pistols' *Great Rock'n'Roll Swindle* movie, only four copies of which are known to have survived – raise higher prices still. Such has been the level of acclaim for Reid's work over the last twenty-five years that his output seems certain to become the province of art connoisseurs as well as rock collectors in the future.

*chapter six*

# PRINTED ARTEFACTS

**left:** Fabulous, *one of the mid-1960s pop magazines that captures all the innocent excitement of the era.*

Even before rock'n'roll music emerged in mid-1950s America, an entire branch of the publishing industry both in the USA and beyond was devoted to popular music. Just as the film world had spawned a wide range of magazine titles, from small-circulation titles for the trade through to mass-market publications built around the latest matinee idols, so the fast-growing music business began to create its own instant library.

Each new phase of pop history, from Beatlemania to punk, and from disco to grunge, created its own purpose-built periodicals to chronicle the latest craze, profile and interview its stars, and capture the spirit of the age in words and pictures. Pop and rock also began to comprise an increasing percentage of the book publishing world from the 1970s onwards, as the teen-oriented titles of earlier years were joined by coffee-table picture books, in-depth biographies, academic critiques, cut-and-paste cash-ins and authoritative histories.

The potential for any collection of printed pop ephemera is endless, as besides the books and magazines you could focus on concert and tour programmes, publicity material, newspapers featuring major pop stories, and much more besides. But, with very few exceptions, the vast majority of this material sells for comparatively small sums. Single copies of even the most obscure or collectible pop and rock magazines from the 1950s or 1960s rarely fetch more than £25 ($37), and more often less than £10 ($15). Fifty pounds, or certainly less than $100, should buy you a copy of all but a handful of pop biographies and other books. A similar price would cover almost all vintage concert programmes and press hand-outs. Like records, printed material offers the collector the chance to build up a fascinating and wide range of material for a modest outlay. But such items only very seldom make it into the catalogues of the major auction houses – with the exceptions detailed in this chapter.

### CONCERT PROGRAMMES

Promoters of concerts and tours usually budget for half of the potential audience at each show to want a souvenir programme to take home with them. Whereas only a handful of posters have usually survived from individual 1950s and 1960s rock concerts, a much larger quantity of programmes has been saved by nostalgic fans. Programmes are easier to obtain than posters, simpler to store and much less likely to become damaged.

Souvenir programmes have altered enormously over the last forty years. Once, they were modestly priced and

*below: A US cinema lobby card for the film* Loving You, *made in 1957, which was signed twice by Elvis Presley.*

simply designed, like the theatre programmes that had been around for decades before them. Their artwork was usually very old-fashioned, with none of the trappings of pop culture that were becoming more apparent on posters and handbills from the same period. They tended to contain very simplistic pen-portraits of the stars, accompanied by the same very conventional publicity photos which had already been seen in magazines and newspapers. The prose was lightweight in the extreme, and might just as easily have been used to talk about a juggling act or a song-and-dance team. But anything that the original buyer may have lost in originality and information is more than matched by their value today as period pieces. Their showbusiness cliches and wonderfully dated advertisements give these early pop concert programmes a charm which is arguably lacking from more modern and professional publications.

These days, programmes are large-format affairs stuffed with lavish colour photography, often including lengthy career histories or critical reassessments of the stars – and sell for almost as much as a concert ticket. The more expensive they are to buy, of course, the less likely they are to be casually thrown away when the concert-goer gets home. As a result, it's unlikely that any tour programmes from the late twentieth or early twenty-first centuries will become valuable collector's items in the foreseeable future – unless, of course, they are signed.

A signature is the magic ingredient that can transform a £20 ($30) programme into a £500 ($750) collectible. Besides the inevitable Beatles artefacts from

1963, filled with autographs collected at the stage door after the show was over, high prices have been paid for a signed Buddy Holly programme from his 1958 UK tour; likewise similar items starring the Rolling Stones, the Who and Jimi Hendrix. Without a signature, collectors will still be interested in all 1950s, 1960s and early 1970s

**right:** *Programmes for concerts promoted by Beatles manager Brian Epstein at his London theatre.*

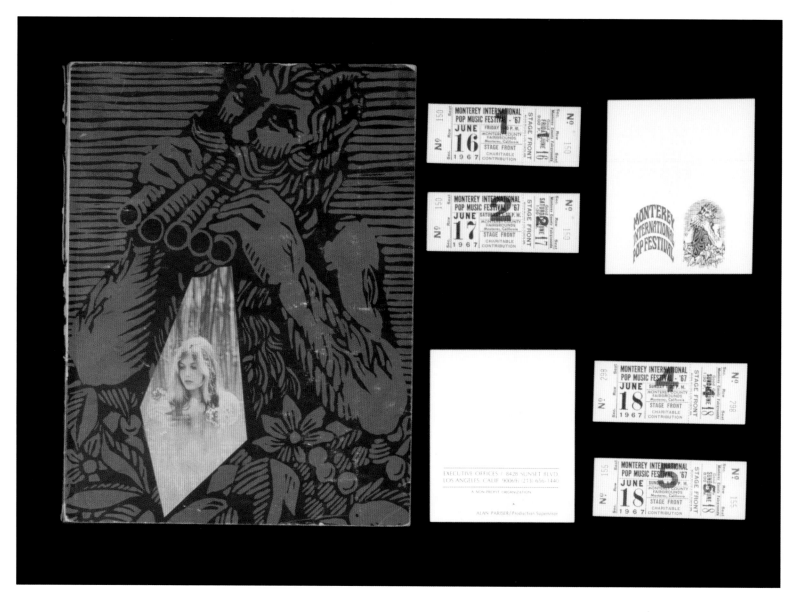

**above:** *A collection of printed ephemera relating to the legendary 1967 Monterey Pop Festival in California.*

concert programmes featuring major (and collectible) artists, from Elvis Presley to the Sex Pistols. Also of great interest are programmes for the package tours, which were the staple diet of the pop industry before the late 1960s, when as many as a dozen stars and budding hopefuls would be crammed onto a single bill, and sent round the country on a cramped bus. Each night they'd play two or three songs before a bunch of hysterical teenagers, before travelling all night and doing exactly the same thing again. It may have been undignified, and sometimes downright dangerous for the performers – many of music's greatest stars, from Buddy Holly and Eddie Cochran to Patsy Cline and Otis Redding, lost their lives in accidents on tour – but for the fan it offered the chance to catch a wide variety of different performers in their prime. There's an obvious fascination today in finding a programme listing a future superstar such as David Bowie or Marc Bolan way down the bill, amongst the mostly forgotten support acts.

If these items appear at auction, then it is likely to be in a job lot, offering (say) twenty programmes from the 1960s for £200–£300 (between $300 and $450). Only a handful of individual tour brochures would ever merit inclusion in a sale at a major auction house without being autographed; and it won't be a surprise to anyone reading this book to discover that they are all related to the Beatles.

In both 1963 and 1964, the Beatles performed a special Christmas Show for their fans at the Hammersmith Odeon theatre in London. Despite the fact that each run lasted for a couple of weeks, programmes from these events have a particular cachet, especially in the USA – perhaps because no such runs of concerts in one venue were ever staged there.

*below: The programme for Buddy Holly's only UK tour, in 1958. Sadly, his reaction to the bizarre cartoon cover isn't recorded.*

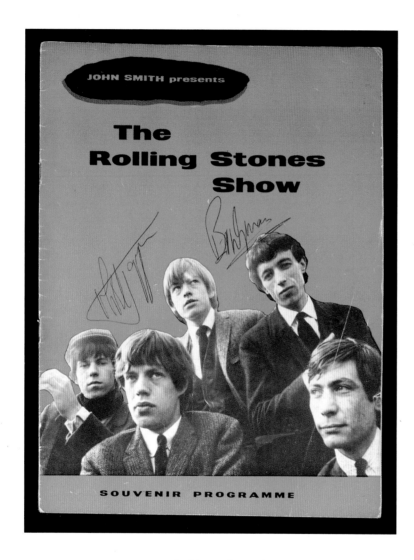

above: *The souvenir programme for a Rolling Stones UK tour in 1964. Mick Jagger signed this copy on several pages.*

More valuable still is the programme from the Beatles' first concert in New York, at the prestigious classical music venue Carnegie Hall, in February 1964. This was a one-off event, attracting a sell-out crowd of around 2,000 people, and very few examples of the special programme produced for the night have survived in anything like perfect condition. It is difficult to speculate how much such an example would sell for, but a dedicated collector would probably be willing to part with in excess of £300 ($450) for such a rarity.

## MAGAZINES AND PERIODICALS

Pop and rock magazines are designed to be immediate, contemporary and out-of-date as soon as the next issue arrives in the shops. At some time or another, most pop fans saved a pile of yellowing copies featuring their teenage obsessions – whether the publication in question is *Fabulous* or *Rave* from the 1960s, *Pop Hits* or *Hit Parader* from the 1970s, or *Smash Hits* from the 1980s and beyond. Almost all of those fans ended up throwing their precious collection away, either when they moved or when parental intolerance of the squalor in their bedrooms reached critical mass.

No doubt a sizeable proportion of those former teenagers have turned around to their parents years later, and complained that they'd be rich if they hadn't been forced to jettison their valuable collection of pop memorabilia. But it's because so many copies met a sorry end that there is a keen market today for complete runs of the most important titles from rock'n'roll's golden eras.

America began to offer its teenagers specialist pop and movie magazines years before the rest of the world realized the potential of this market. Early copies from the mid-1950s rock'n'roll era of titles such as *Dig*, *Datebook*, *Hit Parader*, *16*, *Tiger Beat* and *Teen* can fetch up to $60 (£40) apiece, though understandably the demand for these titles is much bigger in the USA than elsewhere. The debut issue of *Teen* magazine from 1957 sets the scene perfectly: its cover story featured the then recently deceased James Dean, while inside Elvis Presley was deemed to be under threat from a new pop idol, calypso star Harry Belafonte.

All of these magazines survived to chronicle Beatlemania and the mid-1960s pop explosion in the same breathless style, but issues from this period are worth no more than half the price of their counterparts from a decade earlier.

Staying in the USA, the next significant wave of music magazines emerged in the second half of the 1960s, to chronicle the new rock culture and in particular the psychedelic music coming out of California. The earliest of these "serious" rock publications was *Crawdaddy*, founded by the teenage Paul Williams in 1966. All pre-1970 copies of that magazine are collectible, as are titles such as *Big Fat*, *Mojo-Navigator* (which lived and died in 1967), *Vibrations*, *Creem* (especially from 1968 and 1969), *Changes* and *Circus*. The last of these publications survived to chronicle many more eras of rock, but issues from the late 1960s and early 1970s are particularly sought after. In all cases, magazines featuring stars such as Bob Dylan and Jimi Hendrix will usually fetch higher prices than those focusing on more obscure figures.

By far the most collectible US rock paper is *Rolling Stone*, launched in newspaper format by Jann Wenner in late 1967. The four issues published that year could easily sell for a total of £500 (over $750) – although you need to be aware that facsimile copies of issue #1 were later published. Purists reckon that the magazine began to lose its way in the mid-1970s, but the first few years' worth of copies are all of interest to collectors. What's often forgotten is that for several months around 1969 and 1970, a separate

edition of *Rolling Stone* was published in London, replacing some of the US pages with UK-originated features.

British magazines and papers may have been slow to respond to the advent of rock'n'roll, but the UK has always enjoyed a healthy weekly pop press, which has enabled its fans to keep a much closer eye on changing

**right:** *The November 1991 edition of* Rolling Stone *magazine, autographed by its cover stars, U2.*

trends than was possible in the States. Until its recent demise, *Melody Maker* had been chronicling popular music since the late 1920s, gradually shifting its boundaries away from big bands and jazz in time to catch the wave of Beatlemania. The more pop-oriented *New Musical Express* was founded in 1952, and maintained an editorial policy based squarely on the Top 30 singles chart until the early 1970s, when it shifted emphasis towards rock. Sizeable runs of either paper provide a fascinating insight into the day-by-day progress of pop history. Other less popular titles such as *Record Mirror*, *Disc* and (from 1970 onwards) *Sounds* also contributed to Britain's rich culture of rock magazines. These newspaper-format titles were accompanied in the 1960s by the weekly *Fabulous* (mixing stories for teenage girls with pop pin-ups) and the monthly *Rave*, both of which have occasionally cropped up at auction.

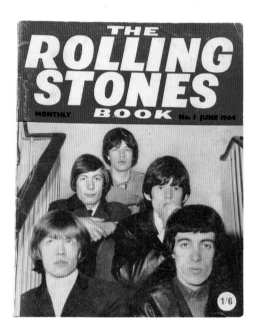

Britain was also unique in pioneering the single-artist monthly fan magazine. *Elvis Monthly* was the first in the field, followed by the shortlived *Billy Fury Monthly*. But

**above:** *The first issue of* The Rolling Stones Book, *the monthly magazine published in London between 1964 and 1966.*

the bestseller was *The Beatles Book Monthly*, issued between 1963 and 1969. It was reissued between 1976 and 1982, but these editions are worth considerably less. The magazine has provided coverage of new Beatle-related activities ever since. Complete runs of 1960s copies of *The Beatles Book* often appear at auction, and sell for between £300 and £500 ($450–$750).

At its peak, *The Beatles Book* was apparently selling more than 300,000 copies a month. *The Rolling Stones Book*, launched by the same publisher in 1964, didn't match those heights, and only survived for thirty issues. But it is more difficult to find today, and a complete run could sell for £200–£300 ($300–$450).

Other fan magazines were devoted to Gerry & the Pacemakers, the Monkees, David Cassidy, Abba (one of the few not published by the Beatles' chroniclers, Beat Publications) and the Police. Sets of *Monkees Monthly* rarely come up for sale, and few collectors have even seen copies of the *Gerry & the Pacemakers* magazine, which only survived for a handful of issues. But neither of these titles could match the prices achieved by the Beatles and Rolling Stones fan magazines.

Probably because the weekly press was so strong, Britain didn't produce any thriving monthly rock magazines in the 1970s, despite the efforts of *Let It Rock* and *Cream*. It was only in the 1980s that titles such as *Record Collector*, *Q*, *Vox* and (a decade later) *Mojo* and *Uncut* became established. Early copies of all of these magazines have sometimes sold for astounding prices – £150 ($225) for the first six issues of *Record Collector*, for instance, or £50 ($75) for the first *Q* – but this success hasn't yet been repeated in the auction room.

**above:** *Teen magazines from the 1960s, such as Fabulous, encapsulated the spirit of the time with their mix of pin-up photographs and features about pop stars.*

Britain's closest equivalents to magazines such as *Crawdaddy* and *Rolling Stone* were probably underground newspapers and magazines such as *International Times* (or *IT*) and *Oz*. These weren't music publications as such, although rock always loomed large in their counter-culture diet of politics, sex and drugs. *Oz* is the prize collectible amongst these titles, with complete sets now fetching well over £2,000 ($3,000). And a similar price was recently achieved by a run of the weekly paper *IT* (although that was for 180 issues, compared to around thirty of *Oz*).

Collectors of rock magazines can find limitless material issued after the early 1970s, ranging from specialist

**above:** *The most valuable pop magazine ever sold at auction. This one-off punk fanzine fetched £564 ($790) in 2001.*

**left:** *A promotional hand-out for the Sex Pistols' debut single in 1976. In 2002, this sold for £528 ($790) in London.*

**opposite:** *The late 1960s produced not just underground papers such as* IT, Ink *and* Friends, *but also the first rock'n'roll fanzines.*

magazines for every imaginable genre to fanzines (particularly sought after from the punk era), and, of course, mainstream pop titles. The New York fanzine *Punk* and British equivalents such as *Sniffin' Glue* are revered by collectors, and it wouldn't be surprising to see collections of magazines like these turning up at auction in the future.

One punk fanzine has already left its mark. In 2001, Christie's sold a copy of *Anarchy In The UK*, the one-off celebration of the Sex Pistols produced in 1976 by Jamie Reid, Sophie Richmond and Vivienne Westwood. Its "official" links with the Pistols' management, its scarcity and the fact that it had been signed by Reid all combined to help it fetch £564 ($790).

### ROCK BOOKS

Guitarist Frank Zappa once declared that "Rock journalism is people who can't write, preparing stories based on interviews with people who can't talk, in order to amuse people who can't read". Many years later, Zappa joined the industry he had once disparaged, when he published his autobiography, *The Real Frank Zappa Book*. The irony is that he needed a ghost-writer to help him do it.

Zappa's cynicism certainly wasn't entirely unjustified, however. Many thousands of books have been published about pop and rock music and musicians over the last five decades, and a large proportion of them have been blatant attempts to cash in on an artist whose career was currently hot. But amidst all the dross, it's possible to build up a library that presents a graphic account of pop history as it happened. Rock books range from autobiographies to reference works, academic critiques to poetry by the stars, photo collections to anthologies of album reviews – and the

**opposite:** *A selection of the many collectible rock books produced in the late 1960s and early 1970s.*

best of them can send you back to the music with renewed enthusiasm and understanding, which is the prime objective of any writing about music.

The earliest pop books were aimed squarely at teenage fans. They offered a mixture of anecdotes culled from publicists' hand-outs, and gentle speculation about the marital plans of singers such as Elvis Presley and Cliff Richard. It was only in 1964, when American journalist Michael Braun spent several weeks on tour with the Beatles, and chronicled the results in a controversial book entitled *Love Me Do: The Beatles' Progress*, that anything resembling adult journalism appeared in a volume about pop.

In less than a decade, rock writing was transformed from the days of *Elvis Presley: Hero Or Heel?* and *Life With Cliff Richard* into a branch of the underground magazine business. Artists such as the Beatles, Bob Dylan and the Rolling Stones commanded full-length biographies, while the first generation of rock critics assembled scholarly work like Paul Williams' *Outlaw Blues* and Richard Meltzer's *The Aesthetics Of Rock*. After Meltzer (who began his book with the unforgettable sentence, "This is a sequel, not a formulation of prolegomena"), there were no barriers left for the aspiring rock writer to climb. Anything could and would be published, from studies of Bob Dylan's links with Judaism to exposés of other stars' less than decent tastes in sex, drugs and rock'n'roll.

Many titles from the first two decades of rock writing can be very difficult to trace in the twenty-first century, but very few would sell for more than the price of a new double-CD. As with magazines and pop papers, it's possible to build up a comprehensive collection for comparatively low cost. Aside from a few specialist dealers, most booksellers have little awareness of which rock books are scarce and which aren't, and bargains are still fairly easy to find.

Some titles simply never turn up, however – and if they did, their price-tag would be staggering. While it's still possible to find a first edition hardback of John Lennon's first book, *In His Own Write*, for £40–£50 ($60–$75), you'll need much more than ten times that amount to locate a copy of the original, privately published collections of poetry by Jim Morrison of the Doors. *The Lords* and *The New Creatures* were later combined into a single volume, but individually they would probably command somewhere between £500 and £1,000 ($750–$1,500) apiece. A similar price could be raised by *Kodak*, a slim 1972 volume by American punk poet Patti Smith. Only one copy is known to be in circulation, and apparently the owner isn't interested in selling!

In terms of books, the two most collectible rock names are the Beatles and Bob Dylan. There are several commercially available Dylan titles from the late 1960s and early 1970s that now change hands for £50 ($75) or more in first edition form, amongst them Daniel Kramer's photo collection and Craig MacGregor's US hardback of *Bob Dylan: A Retrospective*. Amongst the privately published titles, the market leader is Stephen Pickering's *Tour 74*; £300 ($450) wouldn't be a surprising price for this item. Strangely, the next most valuable Dylan title is a mass-market US paperback issued in 1978, when the singer was in the middle of a hugely successful world tour. It should have been impossible for a Dylan title to flop at that point, especially when it was as good as Larry Sloman's *On The Road With Bob Dylan*, but sales in America were disappointing, and the book never made it overseas. As a result, it regularly changed hands for over £100 in the UK, but only around $100 in the US,

although a new edition in 2002 may affect those prices in the future.

Most Beatles-related titles sold in large enough quantities to keep the price down, although collectors still swoon over copies of *The Lennon Play* (a dramatic adaptation of the singer's first two books) and Francie Schwarz's *Body Count* (a kiss-and-tell memoir by a short-term girlfriend of Paul McCartney). *The Beatle Book*, an American title issued with a poster in 1964, is also highly sought after.

The highest prices for any commercially available rock books, however, new or second-hand, belong to the exquisitely produced titles issued by Genesis Publications in England. These leather-bound, hand-tooled volumes are the pinnacle of the publisher's art, and they can sell for as much as £300 ($450) when they are first published. The Genesis catalogue includes the original edition of George Harrison's autobiography, *I Me Mine*, plus the superb memoir by sometime Beatles press officer Derek Taylor, *Fifty Years Adrift*. Both those titles have been sighted at auction, selling for £300–£400 ($450–$600) – not least because all the copies were autographed by Harrison.

Subsequent Genesis titles feature not only the Beatles but also Bob Dylan, the Rolling Stones and Eric Clapton. But their only financial rival to those two Beatles volumes in collecting terms is Michael Cooper's *Blinds And Shutters*, a remarkably lavish collection of photos of, and reminiscences by, the cream of the British rock hierarchy. Each of the 2,000 copies was signed by several rock stars, amongst them members of the Beatles and the Rolling Stones, ensuring that *Blinds And Shutters* will always maintain its value in the auction room.

**left:** *A collection of publicity postcards and photographs signed by the members of Sweden's most successful pop export, Abba.*

# BACKSTAGE PASSES

The process of taking a major rock band on tour produces its own brand of memorabilia. While the audience has to purchase a ticket to enter the arena, members of the crew, entourage, press and even the band themselves need to carry a variety of backstage passes, laminates and other devices signifying that they are allowed access to the hallowed haunts of the dressing-rooms and artists' bars. As Bob Dylan discovered late in 2001, it doesn't matter if you're the star of the show: if you don't display the correct pass to a bouncer or security guard, you won't be allowed backstage. One of the concerts on his US tour came close to being cancelled after Dylan was refused access to his own dressing-room.

Major tours these days spawn many different levels of passes and badges, each allowing its own specific degree of access to the non-public areas of the arena. The ultimate goal is the "access all areas" pass; it's certainly not unknown for roadies and other backroom employees to barter these elusive talismans in return for sexual favours from fans.

Fortunately, auction houses aren't quite so ruthless: they only require you to come up with a little cash. Before a live show, a desperate fan might pay a small fortune for a backstage pass in the hope of meeting their idol. Afterwards, the same item might be worth £10 ($15) as an elitist souvenir. So, like concert programmes, tour passes and badges are only ever sold at auction in bulk.

The same applies in almost all instances to concert tickets and ticket stubs. As usual, however, there are some exceptions to this rule. After the tragic suicide of Nirvana guitarist and lead singer Kurt Cobain in 1994, several auction houses sold unused tickets for the British and European concerts that had been scheduled to take place after his death. Usually, these were mounted with a photograph or autograph of Cobain to enhance their visual appeal.

Collectors have also snapped up tickets (used or otherwise) for a handful of particularly memorable concerts that have passed into rock history. These include the Beatles' last official live performance at Candlestick Park in San Francisco, in summer 1966; the legendary Woodstock Arts & Music Fair festival from 1969; and the Band's farewell concert, known as The Last Waltz, from 1976.

*chapter seven*

# MERCHANDISING

**left:** *A collection of Rolling Stones souvenirs from the 1970s and 1980s, sold as one lot at auction in 1995 for £472 ($700).*

In the 1950s and 1960s, the normal legal contract signed by a singer with a manager, an agent or a record company ran to just one or two pages. Today, entertainment law is one of the fastest growing and most lucrative areas of the legal profession. It's not uncommon for record contracts, or agreements between an artist and a management company, to comprise hundreds of pages of tiny print.

As a result of much more comprehensive contractual arrangements between performers and their managers, agents and record companies, every aspect of an artist's life and work is controlled far more strictly today than in the past. Each agreement is minutely detailed to cover every possible technical innovation via which their music might reach the public, and every potential way in which their name, image and likeness might be marketed and exploited.

It was very different in the early days of rock-'n'roll. When Elvis Presley started out in the mid-1950s, and even when Beatlemania

spanned the globe in 1964, there was very little protection afforded to those artists by law, to prevent their names being applied to any artefact or publication.

Today, every item of memorabilia connected with an artist like Madonna – from badges to posters, photos to videos, lines of cosmetics to fashion ranges – has to be officially approved by her or by her management. Any manufacturer who is caught operating without a licence faces immediate legal action, and the likelihood of bank-breaking damages. That certainly wasn't the case in the past. Throughout the 1950s and early 1960s, pop stars regularly found themselves being targeted by the makers of everything from bubblegum to musical instruments.

The arrival of the Beatles in February 1964 – an event that has passed into US history as "the British invasion" – affected every layer of American society. Politicians and TV pundits competed to work Beatles references into their speeches, and parents and children alike were swept up in the tide of Beatlemania. Manufacturers of novelty goods were quick to take note, and the scale of merchandising and memorabilia that flooded onto the US market was so extreme that it caused the law to be tightened up to prevent a repeat of such gratuitous exploitation.

Even when licences were in place, the Beatles were still in danger of being exploited. Their manager, Brian Epstein, did a remarkable job in steering them from the cellar clubs of Liverpool to international fame. But his naïvety when it came to corporate business affairs was evident when he set up a licensing company in the USA called SELTAEB (or "Beatles" backwards). Under this agreement, the US controllers of the rights to the Beatles' name ended up taking approximately

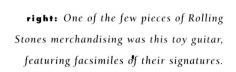

**right:** *One of the few pieces of Rolling Stones merchandising was this toy guitar, featuring facsimiles of their signatures.*

ninety per cent of the money that flooded in from manufacturers, leaving the Beatles with very little indeed, once
their legal fees had been paid. Lots of people became very
rich from Beatlemania merchandising in America – but the
Beatles weren't amongst them.

Besides all the items that were issued bearing the
Beatles' name or pictures, there were many other artefacts
on the shelves in 1963 and 1964 that were obviously targeted at Beatles fans. Some manufacturers used the word
"beetles" in the marketing, or added little beetle logos to

their designs. Others utilized a set of moptop haircuts,
leaving the fans to make the Beatles connection. As memorabilia historians Jeff Augsburger, Marty Eck and Rick
Rann noted, "No doubt the fifteen-year-old fan buying the
'Swingers' nodder dolls thought they were the Beatles.
Long-haired lads, collarless suits, left-handed guitarist,
violin bass, bugs (beetles), 'Yeah, yeah, yeah', etc. would
convey the proper image which the teen would buy."

The result is that there was an almost unbelievable
range of Beatle-related memorabilia and merchandising

**left:** *Part of a massive
collection of promotional
badges that date back to
the 1970s and were sold
at auction in 1995.*

available to the general public in the mid-1960s. British companies began to leap on the rolling bandwagon in the late summer of 1963, after "She Loves You" brought the group to the attention of the national press. Brian Epstein's NEMS management company issued their first official licences to memorabilia manufacturers in November 1963. Then came the real explosion, as Beatlemania took America by storm, and the group visited the USA for the first time in February 1964. British companies were no slouches, but their American counterparts left them cold.

American Beatles expert Barb Fenick, who was the first person to chronicle this memorabilia explosion, wrote two decades ago: "In 1964, Woolworth's had to be Ali Baba's cave. But we didn't know it at the time. Any Beatle fan could walk right in off the street and purchase any of the four Remco Beatles dolls, instruments and all, for under $3.00, less than £2 at that time; Beatles coloring books were only 59 cents (about 40 pence), and all kinds of gaudy necklaces, bracelets, and pins with 'The Lads' lovely faces on them were piled high and going cheap. Lunchboxes, thermoses included, would cost you no more than any other lunchbox in the store. The singles' racks were full of the latest releases, each only 88 cents, picture sleeve and all . . . that we had to pick and choose was the ultimate cruelty. We only had one hardship in those days: poverty!" (*Collecting The Beatles*, Pierian Press, 1982).

In theory, the combination of low retail price, easy access and vast sales should mean that this Beatles memorabilia has very little value to collectors today. In practice, quite the opposite is true. Nobody in 1964 was buying Beatles merchandising with the thought that it might be worth money several decades in the future. These artefacts were selling to highly enthusiastic, sometimes almost hysterical fans – who, by their very nature, were likely to be cavalier in the way they treated their purchases, and fickle about preserving them for posterity.

In many ways, it's the case that the cheaper the item, the less likely it is to have survived. Very few fans bought Beatles bubblegum, for instance, and didn't chew it. Most posters were tacked or taped to bedroom walls, rather than being carefully stored out of the sunlight in cardboard tubes. Toy guitars were strummed, toy drums were bashed, and both usually ended up being broken. Beatles wallpaper was pasted onto walls, not left in pristine condition in its original rolls. Even more expensive items, such as Beatles curtains, almost always suffered from wear and tear. With extremely few exceptions, the only artefacts that survived 100 per cent intact, and (a key point, this) in their original packaging, are those that were abandoned in storerooms or warehouses as bankrupt stock, and then snapped up by some enterprising collector or dealer many years later.

The packaging is often as important to the collector as the item itself. Anyone who's investigated the toy market will know that model cars or trains are worth several times their normal value if they are enclosed in the same cardboard box in which they were sold years earlier. Likewise, Beatles bubblegum is much more collectible wrapped than unwrapped; wallpaper needs to be rolled, not stripped off walls; dolls have to come in their boxes if their true value is to be realized. It's obvious that very few teenagers or preteens caught up in the frenzy of Beatlemania would have had the self-restraint to stop themselves from tearing off the cellophane wrapping and throwing away the box. In fact, they would have been strange Beatles fans indeed if they hadn't done exactly that.

For anyone collecting Beatles memorabilia a certain degree of compromise is necessary unless you have an enormous budget at your disposal. But there's another equally important factor to consider before you start searching for vintage collectibles. After the initial flood of Beatles merchandising between 1963 and 1965, the market rapidly died down as the teenage fans grew up, and their younger siblings transferred their attention to Herman's Hermits, the Monkees or (in the USA, at least) Bobby Goldsboro.

The release of the group's two multi-million-selling compilation albums, *1962–1966* and *1967–1970*, in 1973, coincided with (and undoubtedly helped to boost) a resurgence of interest in the group around the world. Just a few years after their split, the Beatles were starting to inspire nostalgia. Tribute musicals were staged on Broadway and in London's West End, press speculation heightened that the group were about to reunite, and canny manufacturers began to unleash a second wave of Beatles merchandising – which has continued virtually unbroken to the present day.

Much of this second generation material made its 1970s origins obvious. But other items almost exactly mirrored their 1960s counterparts, and only small details – such as the fact that the name of the licensor, always included somewhere on the packaging, was "Apple Corps" rather than "NEMS" or "SELTAEB" – enable collectors to tell them apart from the originals. It is certainly not unknown for dealers to sell these 1970s items as being 1960s originals, whether through ignorance or deliberate deception, and so it is vital to investigate items fully before laying out a large sum.

As with magazines and other printed ephemera, there is no such thing as an uncollectible item of original Beatles merchandising, although values can vary wildly. At one extreme, you can pick up a one-inch badge of the kind available from US bubblegum machines in 1964 for just a few pounds. At the other, you might have to spend well over £1,000 ($1,500) for a pair of "Beatlephones" – headphones designed to plug into a teenager's record-player for intimate listening. The latter price is dependent on the box being intact, however; by themselves, the headphones might only fetch around £200 ($300).

In between those high and low prices, there is literally something for every pocket and every taste. Decorators can bid for Beatles curtains or wallpaper, or perhaps display a Fab Four lampshade or tablecloth. For that important night out, you might want to soak in some Beatles bubble

**below:** *The "tour jacket", which was specially made for Mick Fleetwood to wear at the BRIT Award ceremony in 1989.*

bath, rub yourself down with a Beatles towel (showing the group in Edwardian swimming costumes!) and then apply some Beatles hairspray or Margo of Mayfair talc, before donning a pair of Beatles nylons. Home entertainment could come from a Beatles record player, on which you could play discs stored in a Beatles Disk-Go-Case carrier. You could amuse friends with the legendary Beatles "Flip Your Wig" board game, while passing around thirty-eight-year-old portions of Beatles bubblegum – served off a Beatles tray, of course. A Beatle bedtime can be ensured with some Fab Four pillowcases and a bedspread. Only the natural modesty of the 1960s stopped some enterprising manufacturer from offering a choice of full-size blow-up Beatle dolls for that all-night-long Beatles experience. Sadly, the largest existing model is a mere 33cms (13in) tall.

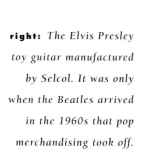

**right:** *The Elvis Presley toy guitar manufactured by Selcol. It was only when the Beatles arrived in the 1960s that pop merchandising took off.*

One particularly popular line of merchandising was the collection of Beatles musical instruments that filled the stores – most aimed at children, not budding musicians. There were about a dozen different guitars displaying various kinds of Beatle-related artwork. These ranged in size and quality from the 35cm (14in) orange model offered by Selcol in the UK, which featured a colour picture of the group on the body, to the 79cm (31in) electric guitar made by the same company in lurid red. This could be housed in a purpose-built cardboard box, which looked more like a coffin than a guitar case.

Of all the merchandising to come out of Beatlemania, however, none has attracted so much attention from collectors in subsequent years as the range of Beatles dolls. As usual, there was more than one design on offer, and prices vary accordingly. The most famous set were made by CarMascot, and went under the title of Bobbin' Head dolls – for the obvious reason that these 20cm-high (8in) figures had their heads mounted on a spring, so that each Beatle would shake his head whenever the car was in motion. But the value of these originals was reduced when facsimile reproductions were made in the 1980s.

CarMascot's biggest rivals in the doll stakes were made by Remco, and were just 12.5cm (5in) tall. Crudely designed (the only distinctive figure was Ringo's, because of his nose), they came in a choice of hard or soft bodies, and both with and without an appropriate miniature musical instrument. Unlike the vaguely lifelike appearance of the CarMascot models, about half the height of Remco's dolls is devoted to their moptopped heads. But you can still expect to have to pay £50 ($70) for each doll, and double that if it is included in its original box.

The *pièce de résistance* of Beatle figurines came in the shape of models that had to be made up from kits, and then hand-painted. They were manufactured by Revell, in both the UK and US, and each Beatle was given his own tag-line by the company's marketing team. George was "Lead Guitar – Loud And Strong"; John was "The Kookiest Of Them All"; Ringo was the "Wildest Skins In Town"; and with Revell's creativity obviously running drier than their paint, Paul was simply "The Great McCartney". If these models were too difficult for fans to colour, however, there was always a Paint-By-Numbers kit for each Beatle ("So great, you'll want to do all four Beatles portraits", as it said on the box).

The merchandising madness knew no bounds, and tens of millions of US dollars (and large quantities of many other currencies around the world) changed hands between fans and manufacturers during the eighteen months between September 1963 and March 1965. Then, just as quickly as it had begun, the memorabilia craze died away almost overnight. The vast majority of these once cherished items were soon forgotten, either being discarded at the time or perishing during a spring-cleaning exercise a few years later. As their owners grew up, their sentimental attachment to their Beatles dolls waned. Fans might keep their records through adolescence and beyond, and maybe their collection of *The Beatles Book Monthly* fan magazines, but items that looked too much like toys were less likely to survive.

Before the Beatles, Elvis Presley had been the first star of the rock'n'roll era to receive the big merchandising treatment. But even the quantity of products associated with "the King" couldn't compare to the flood of Beatles products, and today only the Elvis toy guitars (manufactured by Selcol and sold in a special cardboard box with a sticker) seem to attract much interest at auction. There is certainly nothing of the across-the-board

demand for Presley memorabilia that there is for the Beatles' equivalents.

In the immediate wake of Beatlemania, similar campaigns were launched around the Rolling Stones, but again the impact was minimal. A toy guitar with the printed facsimile signatures of the Stones was sold at auction in 2001 for £329 ($460), but it was a generic children's model, not a piece of official group memorabilia. The

**above:** *A set of Abba dolls, complete with a range of costumes. Sonny & Cher also received the doll treatment in the 1970s.*

Stones were the Beatles' closest rivals in terms of both record sales and publicity during the 1960s, but their merchandising power came nowhere near the Beatles by comparison.

After the Beatles, the next really major group of teen idols to emerge on the global pop scene were the Monkees. Discerning rock listeners greeted their arrival with disdain, complaining that they were "manufactured". The accusation was true, of course, as the group had been recruited to play the role of pop singers in an American TV series. But the group's popularity certainly rivalled that of the Beatles for at least a year, and they continue to command a healthy fan following today.

There was certainly a good deal of Monkees merchandising available in the world's shops during 1967. But the major difference between this campaign and the one involving the Beatles three years earlier was that the Monkees were working under the wings of a network TV company, with the result that all their merchandising rights were sewn up from the start. Far fewer different items were available, and none of them has ever attracted much attention at rock memorabilia auctions.

Since the end of the 1960s, very few artists have been marketed with anything like the range of products associated with the Beatles or the Monkees. Dolls were sold in the image of Abba, and (a far less obvious commercial proposition) the early 1970s incarnation of Sonny & Cher. Both sets do hold kitsch value amongst collectors today.

In the late 1970s, however, a fully fledged hard rock band set out to emulate what their teen pop counterparts had achieved a decade earlier – world conquest by memorabilia overload. The band were Kiss, whose dramatic stage shows and flamboyant (not to mention ridiculous) make-up and costumes made them natural subjects for reincarnation in doll form. Unlike the Beatles, Kiss were utterly in control of their merchandising campaigns, and their products were designed to appeal to the loyalty of both their youngest fans and (with a strong sense of self-parody and irony) their older, denim-clad brothers.

Inevitably, the campaign began with a set of Kiss dolls – one apiece for Gene Simmons, Ace Frehley, Paul Stanley and Peter Criss. The toy guitar made its usual appearance, as did special Kiss microphones, and drumsticks bearing the name of each of Kiss's first two drummers, Criss and Eric Carr. There were Kiss pens, jigsaws, bubblegum, bedspreads, beach towels, sleeping bags, shoelaces and even garbage cans. You could celebrate Halloween with a choice of seasonal Kiss costumes. But by far the most sought-after item of "Kissabilia" was the band's full-size pinball machine, which has been known to sell for more than £1,000 ($1,500). After much initial interest from collectors, however, demand for all these Kiss products has slumped in recent years, once again leaving the Beatles' supremacy in this field unchallenged.

## PROMOTIONAL MEMORABILIA

Almost all of the material under discussion in this chapter was once on open sale to the general public. But there is another entire range of pop and rock memorabilia that is manufactured solely for the purposes of promoting artists and records.

In Chapter Three, we looked at promotional records, which are sent out to the media in the hope that they will either be played on the radio, or discussed in print or over the airwaves. In theory, other promotional items – which can cover everything from baseball caps to leather tour jackets, or ballpoint pens to lavish *objets d'art* – are manufactured and distributed with the same intention. In reality, though, the vast majority of these artefacts are little more than sweeteners to ease the relationship between different sectors of the music industry. Like expenses-paid trips to interview artists, they stop short of bribery, but they are certainly designed to make the media person to whom they are given think kindly of the artists and their record company.

A large percentage of promotional items are very quickly sold on to dealers or specialist collectors, as the record companies are well aware. The result is that there is an immediate surge of interest when the existence of these goodies is first publicized, and in the short term prices can soar. But demand for all but a select few of these items tends to peak very quickly. A good example of this trend is the enthusiasm shown by some collectors for press packs assembled to promote an album by a major artist. These begin to circulate a few weeks before the release date, and often include photos, biographies, a copy of the album and other forms of promotional material, in either printed, CD, video or DVD form. The pack might also include badges, buttons or some more substantial novelty item. It's not uncommon for these to sell for £100 ($150) when they are first produced. But once the album in question has been released, and the immediate demand dies down, the £100 ($150) item can often be found for a third or even a quarter of that price.

Tour jackets are a slightly different matter, as they tend to retain more of their value. They are manufactured

to commemorate a particular series of concerts, and then given to all of the crew who helped the tour happen, plus a number of key media contacts. Like other memorabilia, their value depends on their context: a jacket promoting one of the Rolling Stones' 1970s tours, for instance, will be worth more than a similar item from the 1990s. But it is important to check the source of these jackets, as it is easy for anyone to commission a fake tour jacket from a supplier. Some collectors have been hoodwinked by people purporting to sell jackets from the Beatles' US tours of the mid-1960s, for instance, only to discover that no such articles were ever manufactured at the time.

A handful of promotional artefacts have survived the initial media hype and subsequent lull, and become established collector's items. Amongst them are the Apple Records items mentioned earlier in this chapter; the wall clock, mounted in a wooden box case with a mirrored front, that was made to promote Queen's *News Of The World* album in 1977; and a variety of Sex Pistols material issued that same year, from stickers to badges, and designed by noted punk artist Jamie Reid. This Pistols memorabilia has achieved a cachet beyond anything even connected with the Beatles, and Reid's artwork seems likely to become the stuff of retrospective gallery exhibitions in the decades to come. It's a reminder that sometimes in pop history, the most ephemeral material can turn into high art.

**above:** *Only a handful of media personnel were lucky enough to be sent one of these Queen promotional clocks in 1977.*

*chapter eight*

AWARDS

**left:** *This US multi-platinum award was made to celebrate the success of Madonna's "Ray Of Light" single. Many of these presentation discs were manufactured, and potentially the most valuable would be the one presented to Madonna herself.*

Awards are not just a token of the record industry's appreciation of an artist's talent, but a status symbol in their own right. The offices of record companies, managers, booking agents, music publishers and tour promoters all over the world are lined with gold and platinum discs, Ivor Novello Awards, certificates from publishing organizations like MCPS, BMI and ASCAP, and, in particularly prestigious buildings, Grammy and Brit Awards.

Yet with the exception of Elvis Presley, who devoted a long hallway in his Graceland mansion in Memphis to showing off his many and varied awards, many artists are much more modest, or at least nonchalant, about these trophies. Many stars have casually let slip in interviews that their supposedly cherished gold disc is languishing in the guest bathroom, or propping up a pile of magazines in the basement. Some awards mean more than others, however. Bob Dylan, who has displayed an indifference towards music industry awards throughout his entire career, was apparently so overwhelmed when he was awarded an Oscar in 2000 for the song "Things Have Changed" that he took to carrying round a replica of the award with him on tour, and waving it at his bemused audiences when he performed the prizewinning song.

The worldwide TV screening of the Oscar and Grammy Awards ceremonies ensures that there is plenty of international publicity for the winners. But below that elevated level, there are hundreds of music awards and prizes on offer every year – national ones in most countries; individual ceremonies for television and radio stations; pollwinners' parties for magazines; specialist events for the best artists in blues, country, gospel, folk, jazz and many more recherché

*right: An Ivor Novello award presented to John Lennon for "She's Leaving Home", 1967–68. This award realized £4,275 ($6,400) at auction in 1995.*

genres; and all sorts of industry shindigs celebrating everything from the most-played songs on radio to the best advertising campaigns for new releases.

When an artist is at their creative and commercial peak, awards flood in from all over the world, and it's impossible for even the most sincere performer not to become blasé. The biggest names over the years received innumerable honours and presentations while on tour, and many "local" awards probably ended up being dumped before the visiting stars left the area – not out of spite, but simply because another prize means nothing to someone who is being rewarded every day of their lives.

The result is that a number of stray awards that were handed personally to major pop stars in the 1950s, 1960s and 1970s have turned up at auction. But the auction houses are always extremely careful to check the source of these items. Many stars have lost gold discs and awards to thieves down the years, and so the onus is always on the seller to demonstrate how they got hold of the trophy in question, to ensure that there are no unwelcome legal repercussions to the sale.

In many cases, artists have donated gold discs and other awards to charity auctions, or to give away as prizes in competitions. Anyone who obtains a valuable item in this way should always be sure to retain all the documentation relating to the sale or prizegiving, as it will be very useful should they come to sell the item in the future.

In the hierarchy of awards and trophies, there is no doubt about the top rank: Grammies and Oscars. The Oscars are, of course, the prizes awarded every year by the Academy of Motion Picture Arts and Sciences, but there are keenly fought annual awards for the best film score and for the best original song in a movie. Very few pop and rock songs or soundtracks were nominated for either of

these awards before the 1970s; for instance, the Academy never recognized Elvis Presley movie themes such as "Love Me Tender" or "Jailhouse Rock", or the Beatles' soundtrack albums for films such as *A Hard Day's Night* or *Help!*. In more recent times, however, as pop and rock songs have become an intrinsic part of

**below:** *This gold disc for the Rolling Stones' US single "Ruby Tuesday" was given to the group's guitarist, Brian Jones.*

almost every new Hollywood movie, it has become commonplace for the likes of Elton John or Bruce Springsteen to collect one of the 33cm-high (13in) gold statuettes that are the most coveted awards in American showbiz.

The Grammies also hail from America, and are awarded by the Recording Industry Association of America. Like the Oscar judges, the panel who decided the winners of such categories as Best Rock'n'Roll Song and Best Pop Album took a very conservative approach towards changing styles in the 1950s and 1960s music business. Music that was aimed at teenage audiences was considered too low-brow to be acclaimed by the American record industry, with the result that most of the top awards in the mid-1960s went not to the Beatles, the Rolling Stones or Bob Dylan, but to the likes of Petula Clark (for "Downtown") and the New Vaudeville Band ("Winchester Cathedral"). Once again, this prejudice only began to disappear as the 1960s drew to a close, and since then the Grammies have regularly mirrored (at least, to some degree) critical and commercial success in the rock field.

Few if any Grammy Awards have ever been presented at auction, for the simple reason that they are carefully guarded by their recipients, who realize that these represent the pinnacle of appreciation by their peers. A recent, and very rare, example was the Grammy Award presented to the Beatles for *Sgt. Pepper* that appeared in an on-line auction, finally selling for £130,000 ($195,000), demonstrating that if and when these artefacts appear at auction, the prices easily outstrip those realized by similar awards. For example, if an artist's Brit Award (bestowed by the British recording industry) – or a similar prize from another country – sold for £2,000 (around $3,000), then an Oscar or Grammy could well fetch anything between £5,000 and £10,000 ($7,500 and $15,000) – or even more, if it had been awarded for a particularly legendary song or album. We will have to wait a long time for a rock-related Oscar to appear on the market, however, as recipients have to sign an agreement forbidding them from selling their awards to anyone other than the Academy – who pledge to buy back any unwanted Oscars for a less than generous dollar apiece!

In terms of status, after the Oscars and Grammies come major national awards such as the Brits, and also songwriting awards presented by industry organizations. BMI and ASCAP, the two concerns that control music publishing in the States, regularly hand out lifetime achievement awards, plus certificates and plaques to

*below: The Beatles looking rather unimpressed at being given yet another set of awards in the mid-1960s.*

*right: This US gold disc award for David Bowie's classic Ziggy Stardust LP was presented to his 1970s manager, Tony DeFries.*

right: *In 2001, this silver disc award given to the Bee Gees' record label sold for £329 ($460) at a London auction.*

**right:** *Eric Clapton himself was presented with this British gold single award for "Layla", a memorable track he recorded with his 1970s group, Derek & the Dominos.*

commemorate particularly successful compositions. In Britain, there are the annual Ivor Novello Awards, celebrating the best and most popular songs of the previous twelve months. Musicians usually value these prizes above almost all others, because they are a reward for personal creativity rather than merely public appeal.

Also very highly regarded are the most prestigious awards within particular musical genres – the Country Music Association Awards in Nashville, for example, or the W.C. Handy Awards given to blues musicians in Memphis. Within those tight-knit musical communities, there may actually be more kudos in winning one of these awards than in picking up an Oscar, because the winners of the CMAs and Handys are selected by their peers.

Below these major awards are the hundreds of different prizes on offer around the world, many of which (as we saw earlier) probably mean less to the recipient than to the people who are giving them out. Although there is obviously a vicarious thrill in owning an award presented to Elvis Presley for being the most popular male singer in the Philippines, for example, there is no guarantee that Elvis was ever even aware of the award, let alone saw it or touched it. Once again, this is where the source of an item can make a major difference to its price. If the seller can show that it came directly from the artist or their manager, then that would add substantially to its value.

Similar conditions affect the value of the other major category of award – the gold disc. In fact, there were three varieties of these awards in circulation during the eras that

interest us: silver, gold and platinum discs. The amount of records you had to sell to qualify for each award varied down the years, depending on the territory and the time period. In Britain, for instance, an artist needed to sell 250,000 copies of a single in the 1960s to win a silver disc, and 1,000,000 to gain a gold disc (platinum discs had not been devised then). Those figures were relaxed as the years

Some record companies also pressed their own gold discs to celebrate a particular achievement by their artists.

In terms of collectability, the "official" industry gold discs are much more valuable than those awarded by other commercial organizations. The key words or abbreviations to look for are RIAA (Record Industry Association of America) for the USA and BPI (British Phonographic Institute) for the UK, although once again other countries will have their own equivalents. It's also important to remember that the BPI only began to present "official" awards in 1973, so gold and silver discs from before that date obviously won't carry their logo.

Few people outside the music industry realize that gold discs and their silver and platinum siblings aren't only presented to the artists themselves. Gradually, with each passing decade, the number of gold discs manufactured to celebrate each award has increased. Anyone connected with the success of a particular record – not just the manager, producer, session musicians and engineers, but also PR people and other industry insiders – may be in line to receive an award, even if it's only one manufactured by the record company. The name of the recipient is always engraved on the small plaque mounted alongside each gold disc.

Not surprisingly, values vary enormously according to whose name is on the plaque. A gold disc personally presented to the artist is always worth much more than one given to an unknown outsider. Although it's true that any Beatles- or Elvis-related gold presentation disc is going to have some value at auction, that isn't the case with artists who have made less impact on the pop and rock memorabilia scene. Collectors would happily bid at auction for a Neil Diamond or Tammy Wynette gold disc if their name is on the plaque, for instance, but if the

went by, and gradually the silver disc was phased out. Gold discs then took their place, with the platinum award being instituted for million-sellers. Obviously, the figures were different in every country around the world; in a territory with a much smaller record-buying population, you might only need to sell 50,000 copies to win a gold or platinum disc.

As with other industry awards, there were often several different organizations presenting these gold and silver discs in the 1950s and 1960s. Individual music papers regularly manufactured their own awards, which they handed over to the stars in front of an in-house photographer. The results were displayed proudly to the readers the following week.

**above:** *A white matte gold disc issued by the RIAA in America for the Deep Purple anthem "Smoke On The Water".*

award is made out to a disc jockey or an engineer, bids are likely to be minimal or non-existent.

## BEWARE OF FAKES

Several people over the years have tried to pass off homemade gold discs as the real thing. Many companies offer a quite legal service whereby they will spray-paint any record you give them in gold or platinum, after which you could always choose to mount it and display it on the wall. But without an official plaque, complete with industry logos, to certify their authenticity, items like these are worthless.

Two other myths about gold discs can be dispelled here. First of all, the records in question are never made out of solid gold; at best, they are gold-plated; at worst, they are covered in gold paint. Secondly, the actual record (or these days, the CD) that is covered in gold and then mounted sometime bears no relation to the disc for which the award is being given. Paul McCartney tells the story of how the Beatles once took apart one of their gold disc awards, put the record on the turntable – and discovered that it was actually by their then rivals, the Rolling Stones!

**above:** *This multi-platinum award for the Travis album* The Man Who *illustrates the twenty-first-century shape of presentation discs.*

*chapter nine*

# ARTWORK

From the first time that Elvis Presley appeared on stage and wiggled his hips to the delight of his teenage fans, visual appeal has played a vital role in the rock and pop industry. Iconic record sleeves and photographs have left their mark on posterity, while some musicians have extended themselves beyond music to dabble in many different areas of the visual arts themselves. As a result, everything from John Lennon's doodles to David Bowie's paintings has taken its place in the auction rooms in recent years.

**below:** Back Street Life, *one of the most striking canvases by the Beatles' former bass guitarist, Stuart Sutcliffe.*

A number of British rock stars emerged in the 1960s who had been educated at art school. Often they had chosen that educational route as a way of avoiding the chore of having to take a regular job, or sign up for an academically rigorous course at a university. Discipline was usually lax, the lecturers broad-minded, and to twist an old cliché, art school gave these young musicians a rather bohemian education at the university of life.

Amongst the luminaries who emerged out of the art schools were some of the most influential rock figures of the decade – Eric Clapton, David Bowie, Pete Townshend of the Who, Ray Davies of the Kinks, and, of course, John

Lennon of the Beatles. The art school connection introduced Lennon to the worlds of dada, surrealism and pop art, and allowed him to mingle with fellow students who were experimenting with avant-garde poetry, music and theatre, and investigating the secret powers of certain illicit substances. It was at Liverpool College of Art that John Lennon also met another future member of the Beatles, artist and would-be bass guitarist Stuart Sutcliffe. Their relationship has been chronicled in several books, and also in a hit movie, *Backbeat*.

Sutcliffe was a serious artist, whose immense natural talent is evident from the hundreds of canvases and sketches that he created before his untimely death in 1962, at the age of just twenty-two. Lennon was much less committed to his art, lacking Sutcliffe's dedication to visual creativity and his grounding in technique. Yet he was a vivid and distinctive caricaturist and cartoonist, with a savage, sometimes cruel eye for the macabre. Together, Sutcliffe and Lennon represent an elite of pop and rock artists, who have attempted to be as expressive with a paintbrush or pencil as they are with a guitar or piano.

Lennon's songwriting partner in the Beatles, Paul McCartney, has an artistic bent himself – only expressed in occasional doodles, cartoons and sketches in the 1960s, but exhibited since then via an increasingly sophisticated collection of paintings. Collections of his work have appeared in print, while his art has been exhibited all over the world.

Many pop and rock performers have taken advantage of the opportunity presented by their record sleeves and artwork to exhibit their skills with a brush. Bob Dylan's ultra-naïve daubs on the covers of the Band's *Music From Big Pink* (1968) and his own *Self Portrait* (1970) have become visual icons in their own right – championed by some critics for their simplicity, lampooned by many others for their apparent lack of skill.

The queen of the singer-artists, however, is Joni Mitchell, who began painting her album covers on her self-titled debut album in 1968, and has continued to do so on almost every record she has released since. Unlike Dylan, she has been quite open about her artistic ambitions, staging several well-reviewed exhibitions of her work. On several occasions in recent years, she has described herself as a painter who sings, rather than a musician who paints.

Even more successful in terms of critical approval has been the work of Don Van Vliet – still better known as the uncompromising avant-garde rock performer Captain Beefheart. Like Mitchell, his work first appeared in public on album covers, but since his effective retirement from music in the 1980s, he has worked almost solely as an artist, and his spectacular and often bizarre canvases have garnered glowing reviews from experts who have never heard his music.

Ronnie Wood, whose British rock pedigree includes the Faces and the Rolling Stones, is another guitar-picker who has become a regular contributor to art exhibitions. Unlike Mitchell's almost impressionist style, he specializes in more realist portraits, dismissed by some as caricatures, but applauded by others as capturing the inner spirit of many of his superstar colleagues. And the list goes on: the late Jerry Garcia of the Grateful Dead produced a series of fantasy paintings that won much more praise from his fans than from art-lovers; Tony Bennett, John Mellencamp, Graham Coxon of Blur and Ian Brown of the Stone Roses have diversified into the art world; and David Bowie has become not only a fêted painter, but a patron of the visual arts, financing exhibitions, magazines, books and a website.

With the exception of Stuart Sutcliffe, who is regarded by British art historians as an extremely promising but tragically unfulfilled painter of genuine talent, few of these musicians-turned-artists have left a real impact on the art world. But within the less judgemental confines of the pop and rock memorabilia auctions, original pieces of their art – or indeed limited edition prints – have proved to be very popular with buyers.

As befits the most prominent member of the Beatles, the unchallenged leader in this field is John Lennon. The

**below:** *Rolling Stones guitarist Ronnie Wood demonstrating his second career by putting the finishing touches to a self-portrait.*

outside world was first exposed to his work when he published two books of comedy sketches, nonsense verse and cartoons, *In His Own Write* (1964) and *A Spaniard In The Works* (1965). A third volume, *Skywriting By Word Of Mouth*, was published posthumously in 1985.

Before any of these books were published, however, Lennon's friends and contemporaries in Liverpool had become familiar with his prodigious output of cartoons. He began at school, passing caricatures of teachers around the class, which he occasionally put together in a mock newspaper he called *The Daily Howl*. A particularly striking example of *The Daily Howl*, from the collection of his art college friend Rod Murray, came onto the market in spring 2002. One side of the paper revealed the standard *Daily Howl* format of mischievous news stories and strange drawings; on the other was pasted a watercolour and ink cartoon, similar in style to the work of the much-loved British cartoonist Ronald Searle. Although *The Daily Howl* probably represents the pinnacle of Lennon's juvenile art, dozens of his slapdash cartoons have been offered for sale over the last two decades. Usually, these have been unsigned, but their visual style is unmistakeable. In many cases, their provenance has also been excellent, as they have come from the collection of his former wife, Cynthia Lennon, and were sketched on notepaper bearing the logos of Brian Epstein's NEMS organization or the Beatles' own Apple Corps. Prices for these items have ranged over the last decade from £700 to £8,800, or $1,000 to $13,000.

The most celebrated set of Lennon cartoons, however, is *Bag One*. In February 1969, John's assistant, artist Anthony Fawcett, introduced him to the techniques of lithography. Lennon promised to return in a few weeks with a large collection of drawings that could be issued

were also made available, although these may have been produced without Lennon's approval.

The *Bag One* subscription was quickly taken up, and the original signed sets remain amongst the most sought-after Lennon memorabilia. Infamously, a set of the lithographs was exhibited in London in the early weeks of 1970, only for police to intervene and confiscate several drawings, on the grounds that they were obscene.

**left:** *Paul McCartney has been painting since the 1950s, but only began to exhibit his work in the late 1990s.*

Signed drawings and paintings like the *Bag One* lithographs are easy to authenticate; but auction houses have to take great care to trace the origins of unsigned work. However, well-sourced material by musicians such as Jimi Hendrix, and Charlie Watts of the Rolling Stones has been successfully sold at auction even though it wasn't signed by their creators.

## ALBUM COVERS AND COMMERCIAL ARTWORK

The innate visual appeal of the 12" album sleeve has given hundreds of artists a much larger audience for their work than otherwise would have been the case.

as a limited edition set of lithographs. What no-one anticipated was that the drawings would graphically illustrate his sexual relationship with Yoko Ono, whom he married in March 1969.

By the end of the year, publisher Ed Newman and Fawcett had selected thirteen images and transferred them onto poster-size lithographs, all of which were signed (and numbered, out of 300) by Lennon. They were then sorted into sets of fourteen contained within a special white vinyl carrying case, and sold via subscription. Much later, postcard-sized versions of the same images

The most durable of these sleeve designs have been applauded in their own right, almost regardless of the music that they were intended to house. Peter Blake's celebrated design for the Beatles' *Sgt. Pepper's Lonely Hearts Club Band* (1967), with its massed ranks of the group's heroes and inspirations, has been imitated and pastiched countless numbers of times over the past thirty-five years. In 1981, the lifesize cut-out portrait of the actress Marlene Dietrich that was used for the crowd scene on the cover of *Sgt. Pepper* came up for auction. Signed by Peter Blake, it sold for around £1,300, over $2,500 at that time. Two

*Andy Warhol*

Faith (1969); and countless psychedelic offerings from the Grateful Dead, Jefferson Airplane and Pink Floyd.

Moving into the 1970s, we probably all share a collective memory of the striking imagery of Pink Floyd's *Dark Side Of The Moon* (1973) and *Animals* (1977); the stark black-and-white photo that introduced Patti Smith to the world on *Horses* (1975); the cut-and-paste artwork for *Never Mind The Bollocks, Here's The Sex Pistols* (1978), a Jamie Reid design that seemed to typify punk; and the dramatic onstage photo by Pennie Smith that was the visual centre of the Clash's *London Calling* (1979).

All of these album covers, and many more from the same era, have left a much more indelible mark on their generation and subsequent listeners than any "serious" art produced during that period. Yet each of them was mass-produced in such quantities that they are still freely available to the public for a minimal outlay. But while the records themselves are worth relatively little, the original artwork used to prepare the sleeves can command significant sums, and occasionally it does come up for auction.

It can arrive in several different forms. It could be a blueprint for the finished design, like the quick sketch by Paul McCartney on which he conceived the idea of the legendary *Abbey Road* album sleeve for the Beatles. It could be an original proof of the finished artwork – and sometimes proofs have been sold for albums that never reached the shops, as with several unfinished Rolling Stones projects from the 1960s and 1970s. It could be a printed colour "slick" for the cover, the last stage in the process before the sleeve was printed. Or in an ideal case, an entire portfolio might come up for auction, complete with the photos used on the album sleeve, the typography, sketches and all the other components that went into the final design.

decades later, another *Sgt. Pepper* visual came onto the market – this time for the cut-out of early Hollywood cowboy Tom Mix, which sold for £8,000 ($11,000 plus). The whereabouts of the other figures remain a mystery!

Equally memorable are such 1960s landmarks as the iconic stance of Bob Dylan on his 1965 albums *Bringing It All Back Home* and *Highway 61 Revisited*; the three-dimensional design at the heart of the Rolling Stones' *Their Satanic Majesties Request* (1967); Andy Warhol's stunningly simple banana sleeve for *The Velvet Underground And Nico* (1967); the nude photography of Jimi Hendrix's *Electric Ladyland* (1968) and the solitary album by Blind

**below:** *Original copies of the Velvet Underground's first album are collectible in their own right, but this example was also signed by its designer, Andy Warhol.*

Valuing such items is a difficult process, as each lot is completely different from its predecessor. Obviously, something like the McCartney sketch would fetch many times more than a simple slick for a cover design. But auction houses have to take into consideration the nature of the artefact, the identity of the artists (visual and musical) and the historical stature of the artwork itself.

## ANIMATION

Animated films used to be disparaged as light entertainment for children. But in recent decades, the cartoon films made by companies such as Disney and Hanna-Barbara have finally been recognized as having an intrinsic artistic worth beyond their charm for generations of children of all ages. Entire sales have been devoted to the individual "cels", or images, that are painstakingly created and then combined to create the illusion that these cartoon characters are indeed animated in every sense of the word.

Almost all of these animations are beyond the scope of this book, but there is one music-related cartoon movie that is represented in almost every pop and rock memorabilia auction. In 1967, the Beatles needed to satisfy the demands of their contract with United Artists Films, who required a follow-up to their internationally successful movies, *A Hard Day's Night* and *Help!*. The solution was for the Beatles to "star" in a full-length animated film, entitled *Yellow Submarine*, which was loosely based around their 1966 hit single of the same name. King Features, who had already produced a US cartoon series about the Beatles, were given the job of creating this epic, aided by people such as scriptwriter Erich Segal, who soon became even more famous as the creator of the romantic 1971 movie *Love Story*.

What could easily have been a minor footnote to the Beatles' career instead turned into one of the most acclaimed and enduringly popular animated films ever made. *Yellow Submarine* perfectly caught the visual spirit of psychedelia and the freewheeling, endlessly inventive humour of the Beatles themselves. The most dramatic sequences, such as the re-creation of Liverpool that accompanied "Eleanor Rigby" on the film soundtrack, and the submarine's adventures in the Sea of Holes, were landmarks in animation history.

Many thousands of cels had to be produced for a movie of this length and scope, and choice examples have become highly collectible. The more striking the image, of course, the higher the price; and any cels that feature the cartoon figures of the Beatles, or other favourite characters such as

**below:** *"Ranks of Hammers Goosestepping", a multi-cel set-up on a production background from the animated film,* **The Wall**.

the Blue Meanies and Jeremy Boob, always attract strong bidding. These images are sometimes sold by themselves, against a white background; and sometimes in the context in which they appeared in the film, against a landscape or backdrop of some kind. Once again, the top prices are produced by the most striking images.

Some cels have also emerged in recent years from the cartoon series *The Beatles*. This was a far less interesting enterprise than *Yellow Submarine* on every level: it was visually conservative, dramatically banal and featured no personal input from the Beatles themselves, who distanced themselves from the project as much as they could. But cels featuring their cartoon images still have a following amongst collectors, although not on the same scale as the more attractive *Yellow Submarine* designs.

The only rock-related animation to rival the Beatles' efforts was *The Wall*, the superb feature film based around the theme and songs of Pink Floyd's 1979 hit album. The original illustrations for the cover artwork of the record, and the characterizations for the film, were drawn by the renowned British cartoonist Gerald Scarfe. In 1990, Christie's staged a special auction of animation cels from the movie of *The Wall*, to coincide with the all-star performance of the album that was organized by Floyd composer Roger Waters in Berlin. Individual cels from that sale have often reappeared at auction, and generally fetch similar prices to those raised by all but the most appealing *Yellow Submarine* cels.

## PHOTOGRAPHS

Many of the album covers discussed earlier in this chapter have centred around photographs that have encapsulated the appeal and image of a major artist. In their very different ways, the portraits of the Beatles on the 1963 LP *With The Beatles* (taken by Robert Freeman) and Patti Smith on her 1975 LP *Horses* (by Robert Mapplethorpe) provided a brilliant summary of the artists' appeal at that moment in their careers, and did almost as much to establish them in the public eye as the music they were designed to accompany.

Pop and rock have always depended on striking visual images, and few stars have ever survived long on music alone. Even the most cerebral performers, such as Bob Dylan, Leonard Cohen and Joni Mitchell, quickly realized the importance of controlling the way in which their portraits reached the public.

Over the last five decades, music has spawned its own galaxy of star photographers, who have captured the most important icons for posterity. These lensmen and women regularly see their work collected inside hard covers, and treated with the same reverence as top Hollywood lensmen. In different ways, American names such as Annie Liebowitz and Jim Marshall, and British photographers such as Pennie Smith and Jill Furmanovsky, have made as sizeable a contribution to rock culture as many of the performers whom they have portrayed. From an earlier age, photographers such as Dezo Hoffmann and Harry Hammond encapsulated the appeal of the 1950s and 1960s in unforgettable black-and-white images that survive as potent visual records of those decades. Society, celebrity and Hollywood photographers have also taken their share of rock portraits, of everyone from the Beatles to Madonna.

In recent years, photography has taken its deserved place in the calendar of fine art auctions, and choice examples have raised phenomenal prices on both sides of the Atlantic. Photographs also form a small but very important part of the pop and rock memorabilia market, with collectors choosing to focus on anything from fans' snapshots of concerts or chance encounters with their idols, to limited signed prints of classic images.

The music business is awash with promotional photos: for the past fifty years, no new artist has been launched without the accompaniment of glossy black-and-white or colour pictures, traditionally known as "ten-by-eights" (10 x 8in, or about 25 x 20cm). These can be sent out to the media in their thousands, and as a result they rarely sell for more than a few pounds apiece – unless, of course, they are autographed, as described in Chapter Two.

Equally common are pictures taken by fans, which can be both fascinating and revealing – catching stars outside the airbrushed, cosmetic world of the photo studio. Once again, though, these photographs have little financial value, unless they are of high quality and are being sold with copyright, which would give the purchaser the chance to exploit them commercially. Without copyright, they raise marginally more at auction than the standard press photograph.

Occasionally, collections of unpublished pictures by professional photographers surface at auction, and these attract far more attention from both collectors and media organizations. Despite the fact that they were captured on film all over the world, there is obviously only a finite number of photographs of the classic rock artists of the 1950s and 1960s in existence. The chance to purchase a few rolls of previously unseen shots of the Doors, for example, or Jimi Hendrix, can spark a furious bidding war. Once again, the magic ingredient is copyright, which translates already attractive artefacts into a potentially lucrative investment.

The final class of photographs to surface at auction are the limited edition prints, signed by the photographer

(and, on very rare occasions, signed by the subject as well). They are often mounted on card or within a frame, and accompanied by a description and perhaps a studio stamp, besides the lensman's signature.

A word of caution should be applied, even in this area, however. Unlike a limited edition art print or a numbered run of a rare book, there is nothing finite (or definitive, for that matter) about these images. The

**above:** *One of the most dramatic images from a set of Bowie photos taken by Mick Rock in the early 1970s and sold in 2002.*

signed prints are usually created many years after the original photograph was taken, and there is nothing to prevent the cameraman from creating another "limited" run whenever he pleases in the future. Though they are attractive to display, many of these images are prepared in very lengthy editions, and therefore lack the exclusivity that is the hallmark of all the really valuable items of pop and rock memorabilia.

# DAVID BOWIE AS A VISUAL ARTIST

In recent times, David Bowie has challenged John Lennon's eminence amongst the ranks of multi-media artists from a musical background. His well-documented obsession with the visual arts – which has been evident in his chameleon-like shifts of image ever since the mid-1960s – has matured over the years. Bowie has a masterful collection of modern British pictures and sculpture, and more recently has become an instrumental patron of the so-called Britart movement. In the literary field, Bowie is a founder of the critical magazine *Modern Painters* and its publishing cousin 21 Publishing. He has also championed the sponsorship of young artists, using his own much-visited website, Bowieart.com, as a major medium.

Bowie has devoted a lot of energy to his own personal artistic endeavours over the past thirty years. One of his first series of prints from the mid-1970s is the *Tarot Minor-Arcana*, a set of five serigraphs (silk screen images) on fine pressed rice paper depicting images from the Tarot (Death, Love, Star, Earth and Moon). These prints were first produced in 1975, and in 1995 Bowie reworked them into an extremely popular limited edition print. Some nineteen years after the *Tarot Minor-Arcana* was originally created, one of those precious rice paper sets was sold at Christie's for £4,800 ($6,800).

The majority of Bowie's limited edition computer print work dates from the 1990s. *The Alder Diaries* is a collection of seventeen mixed media computer-generated prints from 1994. In 1997, a set was purchased at Christie's for £2,070 (nearly $3,000). Back in 1994, Bowie also created a series of prints called *We Saw A Minotaur*: the fourteen prints in a hand-made box relay the mythical story of a play written by Jon Ve Sadd (a word play on David Jones, Bowie's real name). Each set was signed and numbered by the artist, and included a hand-coloured frontispiece. Created in an edition of fourteen, only five sets were completed, one of which sold at Christie's for £6,300 ($9,000) in 1997.

Rarer still are Bowie's sculptures. *The Remember Series* features chrome-plated bronze renderings of African animals inspired by a treasured set of Kenyan chess pieces. The edition ran to just eight sets in 1995, and has yet to appear at auction. In fact, most of Bowie's work remains with private and public collectors, and little has yet come to auction. The few limited edition prints and sculptures barely scratch the surface of Bowie's prolific output – his paintings, drawings, installations, sculptures, wallpaper and computer-generated prints are an ongoing passion.

# COLLECTORS' INFORMATION

# Collectors' tips

Whether you are buying expensive guitars or ephemeral items of pop merchandising, there are several basic rules that it is important to remember.

### PROVENANCE

For any rare item, especially anything with a personal connection to a major artist, details of its provenance, or origin, can be absolutely vital. Wherever possible, such items are sold with letters of authenticity stating the circumstances in which they were obtained, and how (if it is not immediately obvious) they are linked to the artist in question. In the case of stage costumes, instruments and personal effects, photographs of the artist using or wearing the item can also be used to authenticate them.

### ORIGINALS AND REPRODUCTIONS

Many items of pop and rock memorabilia, from records and posters to ephemeral fan novelties, have been produced in more than one edition, often separated by decades. While in some cases the price differential between them can be minimal, more often an original will be worth many times the value of a later reproduction. Some later editions of records and other memorabilia clearly advertise their "reissue" status; others are much more complex to identify. In all cases, there is no substitute for expert knowledge, or at the very least basic research, before you buy.

### CONDITION

In all areas of collecting, the condition of an item can substantially affect its value. A rare record that is worth, say, £1,000 ($1,500) in perfect ("mint") condition may be worth no more than £50 ($75) if it is very badly scratched, chipped, cracked or even broken. Similar differentials apply throughout the collecting field, although it is a general rule of thumb that the rarer and more exclusive the item, the more lenient a buyer is likely to be towards at least some degree of wear and tear.

### PACKAGING

Items of vintage pop and rock memorabilia require as much of their original packaging to be intact as possible. Records should come with their original sleeves and inserts; books with their dust-jackets; merchandising novelties with their cardboard or plastic boxes; even bubblegum packs with their cellophane wrappers. In all these cases, the absence of the packaging will substantially affect the value of the item.

# Top ten highest priced sale items

## TOP TEN AUTOGRAPH MATERIAL

1  **John Lennon** – *a six-page handwritten draft letter to Paul and Linda McCartney, c. 1970–71, £51,150 ($71,600), Christie's London, 2001.*

2  **The Beatles** – *signed copy of the LP* Sgt. Pepper's Lonely Hearts Club Band, *£39,950 ($59,900), Sotheby's London, 2002.*

3  **John Lennon** – *a rare autographed manuscript page from the* Daily Howl *with a scarce cartoon sketch titled "Keen Type" to the reverse, c. 1957, £32,900 ($49,300), Christie's London, 2002.*

4  **The Beatles** – *a rare autographed copy of the album* Rubber Soul, *1965, £25,850 ($36,560), Sotheby's London, 2002.*

5  **The Beatles and Tony Sheridan** – *a rare early musicians' salary receipt for an appearance at the Top Ten Club, Hamburg, May 1961, signed by John Lennon, Paul McCartney, George Harrison, Stuart Sutcliffe, Pete Best and Tony Sheridan, £18,800 ($27,392), Christie's London, 2002.*

6  **Elvis Presley** – *a three-page handwritten letter from Presley to girlfriend Anita Wood, 1958, £14,100 ($20,727), Christie's London, 2001.*

7  **John Lennon and Yoko Ono** – *a self-portrait caricature by Lennon of himself and Ono, signed and inscribed, c. 1968, £12,925 ($18,832), Christie's London, 2002.*

8  **The Beatles** – *a rare Swedish concert poster signed by all four Beatles, 1963, £11,750 ($17,272), Christie's London, 2001.*

9  **The Beatles** – *an LP,* Please Please Me, *signed by all four Beatles, New Zealand, Mono, 1963, £11,750 ($17,272), Christie's London, 2002.*

10  **Paul McCartney** – *the official press statement devised by Tony Brainsby following the death of John Lennon, with deletions and alterations in McCartney's hand, 9 December 1980, £11,500 ($18,400), Christie's London, 1997.*

## TOP TEN LYRICS SOLD AT AUCTION

1  **Paul McCartney** – *"Getting Better", 1967, £161,000 ($241,500), Sotheby's London, 1995.*

2  **John Lennon** – *"If I Fell", 1964, $171,000 (£117,900), Christie's US, 2001.*

3  **Paul McCartney** – *"Hey Jude", contained in a notebook belonging to Mal Evans, 1967, £111,500 ($178,400), Sotheby's London, 1998.*

4  **John Lennon** – *"I Am The Walrus", handwritten, 1967, £78,500 ($125,600), Christie's London, 1999.*

5  **John Lennon** – *"Plastic Ono Band", twelve pages of lyrics for the album, 1970, $102,800 (£70,900), Christie's US, 2000.*

6  **Paul McCartney** – *"Ob-la-di Ob-la-da", handwritten, 1968, £29,900 ($44,850), Sotheby's London, 1995.*

7  **Jim Morrison** – *"Moonlight Drive" and "We Could Be So Good Together", handwritten on both sides of a single sheet of paper, £21,620 ($34,600), Sotheby's London, 1998.*

8  **John Lennon** – *"Instant Karma", typescript with handwritten annotations and additions, 1970, £23,000 ($36,800), Christie's London, 1997.*

9  **George Harrison** – *"Piggies", handwritten, 1968, $23,500 (£16,800), Christie's US, 2001.*

10  **Jimi Hendrix** – *"Coming Down Hard On Me Baby", handwritten, 1970, £10,500 ($16,800), Sotheby's London, 1997.*

## TOP TEN RECORDINGS INCLUDING: REEL-TO-REELS, ACETATES, INTERVIEWS, FILMS AND RARE RECORDS (WHITE ALBUMS ETC.)

1  **The Quarry Men** – *a rare reel-to-reel recording of the Quarry Men at St Peter's Church Hall, Woolton, Liverpool, 6 July 1957, £78,500 ($117,750), Sotheby's London, 1994.*

2  **John Lennon** – *two previously undocumented recordings of Lennon with his step-daughter, Kyoko Cox, 1969, £75,250 ($109,639), Christie's London, 2002.*

3  **John Lennon** – *a previously undocumented recording of Lennon developing the lyrics and melody to "She Said, She Said", 1966, £58,750 ($85,599), Christie's London, 2002.*

4  **Rolling Stones** – *a rare reel-to-reel recording of Mick Jagger and Keith Richards at home, 1962, £78,500 ($117,750), Christie's London, 1994.*

5  **The Beatles** – *unreleased footage taken by Tony Barrow on US tour, 1965, £26,400 ($37,600), Christie's London, 1986.*

6  **The Beatles** – *the Beatles in Bournemouth, 1963, £25,300 ($40,500), Christie's London, 1998.*

7  **Lennon and Ono** – *interview with Richard Thompson, 1971, £23,500 ($34,239), Christie's London, 2002.*

8  **The Beatles** – *a rare double-sided acetate of the Beatles live at The Cavern Club, September 1962 – Some Other Guy/Kansas City, £16,050, ($24,000), Christie's London, 1993.*

9  **Yoko Ono and John Lennon** – *a rare single-sided acetate "Don't Worry Kyoko", previously undocumented with significant variations to the released version, accompanied by a letter from Yoko to her daughter, Kyoko, £9,400 ($14,000), Christie's London, 2002.*

10  **The Beatles** – *home-movie footage of filming of Magical Mystery Tour, 1967, with copyright, £9,200 ($14,500), Christie's London, 1999.*

## TOP TEN INSTRUMENTS AT AUCTION

1  **John Lennon** – *piano used to compose "Imagine", £1,500,000 ($2,250,000), Fleetwood Owen, London, 2000.*

2  **Jerry Garcia** – *custom-made guitar "The Tiger", $850,000 (£566,500), Guernsey's US, 2002.*

3  **Jerry Garcia** – *custom-made guitar "The Wolf", $700,000 (£466,500, Guernsey's US, 2002.*

4  **Eric Clapton** – *"Brownie", 1954 Fender Stratocaster, $497,500 (£316,879), Christie's US, Eric Clapton's Guitars, 1999.*

5  **Jimi Hendrix** – *white Fender Stratocaster, £198,000 ($316,800), Sotheby's London, 1990.*

6  **John Lennon** – *late 1950s Gallotone "Champion" acoustic guitar, £155,600 ($249,000), Sotheby's London, 1999.*

7  **Buddy Holly** – *Gibson guitar, $242,000 (£151,250), Sotheby's US, 1990.*

8  **Eric Clapton** – *1954 Fender Stratocaster, $211,500 (£134,713), Christie's US, Eric Clapton's Guitars, 1999.*

9  **Eric Clapton** – *1974 Martin 000-28 acoustic guitar, $173,000 (£110,191), Christie's US, Eric Clapton's Guitars, 1999.*

10  **Jimi Hendrix** – *1966 black Fender Stratocaster, £100,000 ($160,000), Sotheby's London, 1997.*

## TOP TEN STAGE COSTUME/PERSONAL WARDROBE AT AUCTION

1   Elvis Presley – *"Aloha" stage cape, 1972, $105,250 (£66,000), Guernsey's US Archives of Graceland sale, 1999.*

2   Elvis Presley – *black-and-green stage jumpsuit, 1971, $82,250 (£51,500), Guernsey's US Archives of Graceland sale, 1999.*

3   Geri Halliwell – *Union Jack stage outfit, worn for Brit Awards 1997, £41,320 ($66,112), Sotheby's London, 1998.*

4   Elvis Presley – *sleeveless stage jumpsuit with matching jacket and belt, 1975, $46,000 (£28,750) Guernsey's US Archives of Graceland sale, 1999.*

5   Jimi Hendrix – *oriental-style jacket, c. 1967, £30,000 ($45,000), Sotheby's London, 2000.*

6   George Harrison – *pair of black leather ankle boots c. early 1960s, signed by Harrison later, $41,117 (£27,400), Lelands Internet US, 2002.*

7   Elvis Presley – *"Burning Love" stage cape, 1972, $40,250 (£25,150), Guernsey's US Archives of Graceland sale, 1999.*

8   Jimi Hendrix – *peacock feather waistcoat, 1967–68, £24,150 ($36,225), Sotheby's London, 1995.*

9   John Lennon – *tan suede jacket worn on cover of* Rubber Soul, *1965, £20,250 ($30,350), Christie's London, 1995.*

10  Elvis Presley – *black voile flowery shirt worn in "That's The Way It Is", 1970, £19,550 ($31,250), Christie's London, 1999.*

## TOP TEN JEWELLERY/PERSONAL EFFECTS AT AUCTION

1   Elvis Presley – *Walther PPK 9mm handgun, $116,750 (£73,000), Guernsey's US Archives of Graceland sale, 1999.*

2   Buddy Holly – *black wire rim glasses, c. 1957, $45,000 (£30,000), Sotheby's US Buddy Holly Estate sale, 1990.*

3   Elvis Presley – *prescription sunglasses with gold frame, 1971, $37,375 (£25,775), Guernsey's US Archives of Graceland sale, 1999.*

4   Elvis Presley – *Hamilton electric wristwatch, $37,375 (£25,775), Guernsey's US Archives of Graceland sale, 1999.*

5   Elvis Presley – *"The Living Bible", Tyndale House publishers, bound in blue leather, c. 1970s, $28,750 (£19,827), Guernsey's US Archives of Graceland sale, 1999.*

6   Jimi Hendrix – *a Bobby Lee Co. guitar strap, 1970, £4,675 ($7,950), Sotheby's London, 1991.*

7   Elvis Presley – *a custom-made ring modelled as a jaguar's head, the mouth and eyes set with navette-cut rubies, £4,620 ($7,400), Christie's London, 1990.*

8   John Lennon – *glasses with gold-coloured frame, with yellow-tinted prescription lenses, c. 1967–70, £4,255 ($6,350), Sotheby's London, 1995.*

9   John and Cynthia Lennon – *address book from 1967, £3,850 ($6,500), Christie's London The Cynthia Lennon Collection, 1991.*

10  Jimi Hendrix – *a sterling silver ring of Celtic design, c. 1967, $5,405 (£3,727), Christie's US, 2000.*

## TOP TEN CARS SOLD AT AUCTION

1. **John Lennon** – *1965 Rolls-Royce Phantom V limousine, £1,768,462 ($2,652,700), Sotheby's London, 1995.*
2. **Sir Elton John** – *1993 Jaguar XJ220, £234,750 ($330,763), Christie's London The Collection of Sir Elton John, 2001.*
3. **Sir Elton John** – *1973 Rolls-Royce Phantom VI Limousine, £223,750 ($317,264), Christie's London The Collection of Sir Elton John, 2001.*
4. **Elvis Presley** – *1956 Lincoln Continental Mark II, $295,000 (£184,350), Guernsey's US Archives of Graceland sale, 1999.*
5. **Sir Elton John** – *1956 Bentley S1 Continental Fastback, £196,250 ($276,516), Christie's London The Collection of Sir Elton John, 2001.*
6. **Sir Elton John** – *1994 Bentley Continental Convertible, £163,250 ($230,019), Christie's London The Collection of Sir Elton John, 2001.*
7. **John Lennon** – *1970 Mercedes-Benz 600 Pullman Limousine, £137,500 ($220,000), Christie's London, 1989.*
8. **Sir Elton John** – *1985 Aston Martin V8 Vantage Coupe, £102,750 ($144,775), Christie's London The Collection of Sir Elton John, 2001.*
9. **Sir Elton John** – *1987 Aston Martin V8 Vantage Volante, £101,650 ($143,225), Christie's London The Collection of Sir Elton John, 2001.*
10. **Sir Elton John** – *1992 Ferrari 512 TR, £89,550 ($126,176), Christie's London The Collection of Sir Elton John, 2001.*

## TOP TEN CONCERT/PROMO POSTERS AT AUCTION

1. **The Beatles** - *hand-painted poster for the Kaiserkeller in Hamburg, 1960, £17,480 ($26,250), Sotheby's London, 1996.*
2. **Elvis Presley** – *an early concert poster for an appearance by Presley, and others, at the Grand Ole Oprey, 1955, New City Auditorium, Florida, $12,650 (£7,900), Sotheby's US, 1998.*
3. **The Beatles** – *a concert poster for an appearance at The Town Hall Ballroom, Abergavenny, Wales, 1963, £6,462 ($1,062), Sotheby's London, 2002.*
4. **Various artists** – *A rare concert poster for Carnegie Hall, November 14, 1952, line-up includes: Duke Ellington, Billie Holiday, Charlie Parker and Dizzy Gillespie, £4,950 ($7,400), Christie's London The Chan Parker Collection, 1994.*
5. **The Beatles** – *a concert poster for an appearance at the Gaumont, Ipswich, May 1963, £4,700 ($6,815), Christie's London, 2000.*
6. **The Beatles** – *hand-painted poster for an appearance at The Cavern Club, early 1960s, $6,325 (£4,200), Sotheby's US, 1994.*
7. **The Beatles** – *"The Beatles Christmas Show" poster, 1963–64, Hammersmith Odeon, London, £3,680 ($5,900), Christie's London, 1998.*
8. **The Sex Pistols** – *a concert poster for "A Mid-Nite Special" at the Screen on the Green, 1976, £3,525 ($5,300), Christie's London, 2000.*
9. **The Beatles** – *concert poster for an appearance in Harrogate, 1963, £3,450 ($5,175), Sotheby's London, 1994.*
10. **The Jimi Hendrix Experience** – *Swiss concert poster, "Monster Konzert", Zurich, 1968, £3,290 ($4,600), Christie's London, 2001.*

## TOP TEN MERCHANDISE SOLD AT AUCTION

**1**    **The Beatles** – *a Selcol Beatles Jnr. toy guitar in original packaging, £3,450 ($5,100), Christie's London, 1999.*

**2**    **The Beatles** – *record player, 1960s, $4,887 (£3,250), Sotheby's US, 1995.*

**3**    **The Beatles** – *a set of four wall plaques modelled as portraits of the four individual Beatles by Kelsboro Ware, c. 1964, £2,070 ($3,100), Christie's London, 1996.*

**4**    **The Beatles** – *a Selcol "Beatles Red Jet Electric" toy guitar, with Granada 4 toy amp, c. 1964, £1,762 ($2,554), Christie's London, 2001.*

**5**    **The Beatles** – *a set of four "Bobbin Head" character dolls by Car Mascot Inc., in original box, 1964, £1,057 ($1,532), Christie's London, 2000.*

**6**    **The Beatles** – *a set of four glass Christmas tree decorations modelled as the four Beatles, c. 1964, £977 ($1,400), Christie's London, 1996.*

**7**    **The Beatles** – *five "Long Eating Licquorice Records", by Clevedon Confectionery, with original box, c. 1964, £920 ($1,334), Christie's London, 1996.*

**8**    **The Beatles** – *an uncut sheet of "Ringo Roll" cellophane wrapper, c. 1964, £920 ($1,334), Christie's London, 1998.*

**9**    **The Beatles/The Monkees** – *an American novelty gum ball dispenser, c. 1964, £880 ($1,320), Christie's London, 1994.*

**10**    **The Beatles** – *a set of four glass gold-rimmed tumblers by Joseph Lang & Company, c. 1964, £805 ($1,167), Christie's London, 1998.*

## TOP TEN AWARDS AT AUCTION

**1**    **The Beatles** – *Grammy for Sgt Pepper presented to the Beatles, 1967, $130,000 (£86,500), Sotheby's Internet, 2002.*

**2**    **The Beatles** – *an in-house gold disc presented to the Beatles for Sgt Pepper, 1967, £14,300 ($21,450), Sotheby's London, 1982.*

**3**    **The Beatles** – *RIAA gold disc, white matte, presented to the Beatles for "I Want to Hold Your Hand", 1964, $11,162.*

**4**    **The Beatles** – *RIAA gold disc, white matte, presented to the Beatles for "Hey Jude", 1968, $11,000 (£7,350), Sotheby's Internet, 2002.*

**5**    **The Rolling Stones** – *RIAA gold disc, white matte, presented to Mick Jagger for "Out Of Our Heads", 1965, £6,900 ($10,000), Sotheby's London, 1998.*

**6**    **The Who** – *RIAA gold disc, presented to Peter Townshend for "Tommy", £6,462 ($9,000), Sotheby's London, 2001.*

**7**    **The Beatles** – *RIAA gold disc, white matte, presented to the Beatles for "Can't Buy Me Love", £5,288 ($7,400), Sotheby's London, 2001.*

**8**    **Elvis Presley** – *RIAA gold disc, white matte, presented to Elvis Presley for "Elvis-Aloha From Hawaii via Satellite", £4,700 ($7,520), Christie's London, 1995.*

**9**    **John Lennon** – *an Ivor Novello award for "She's Leaving Home", 1967–68, £4,275 ($6,412), Christie's London, 1995.*

**10**    **The Rolling Stones** – *RIAA gold disc, white matte, presented to Mick Jagger for "Through The Past Darkly", £4,230 ($6,350), Sotheby's London, 2002.*

## TOP TEN ARTWORK

**1** **Peter Blake/The Beatles** – *artwork for the drumskin featured on the album cover* Sgt Pepper, *1967, £52,100 ($78,150), Sotheby's London, 1994.*

**2** **John Lennon** – Bed-In *sketch, £27,000 ($43,200), Sotheby's London, 1997.*

**3** **John Lennon** – *a collage of magazine cuttings, 1974, signed, dated and titled "John Lennon October 1st 1974 Benny and the Jets", £23,100, ($36,950), Sotheby's London, 1990*

**4** **John Lennon** – *complete set of* Bag One *limited edition lithographs, £13,800 ($20,700), Sotheby's London, 1995.*

**5** **John Lennon** – *original manuscript pages for* The Daily Howl, *c. 1957, £13,200 ($21,100), Sotheby's London, 1988.*

**6** **The Beatles** – *original artwork from the rear luggage door of the* Magical Mystery Tour *bus, 1967, £11,270 ($16,900), Sotheby's London, 1995.*

**7** **John Lennon** – *complete set of* Bag One *limited edition lithographs, £8,280 ($12,400), Christie's London, 1996.*

**8** **Charlie Parker** – *self-portrait sketch, £5,500 ($7,700), Christie's London The Chan Parker Collection, 1984.*

**9** **Paul McCartney** – *concept sketch for the album cover* Give My Regards To Broad Street, *1984, £4,600 ($6,900), Sotheby's London, 1995.*

**10** **The Beatles** – *an original watercolour production background from* The Yellow Submarine, *1968, £4,465 ($6,250), Christie's London, 2001.*

*These lists are as up to date as possible but are for guidance only and are not definitive.*

# Glossary

### ACETATES

These discs, pressed on lacquer, which is much thicker and more easily damaged than vinyl records, were pressed in very small quantities to allow artists, producers, journalists, etc. to hear a newly completed recording of a song. In the days before cassette tape became a standard household item, engineers cut a handful of acetates at the end of a recording session, for the artists to review their progress. These discs almost always had white labels pasted onto them, with the track information either handwritten or typed on the labels. Their prime attraction to collectors is the fact that they often feature otherwise unobtainable versions or mixes of songs.

### BOOTLEGS

Since the late 1960s, individuals and underground companies have manufactured illicit records and (more recently) CDs by major artists, featuring live or studio material that wasn't intended for release. Artists such as the Beatles and Bob Dylan have been subject to several thousand of these bootleg releases, which are keenly sought after by diehard fans. Artists and their official record companies generally frown upon these releases, as they receive no royalties from their sale, and have no control over their contents. Many successful court actions have taken place to halt the making and selling of bootleg records, which is illegal in almost every country in the world, but the under-the-counter trade still continues.

### CELS

Cels are the celluloid sheets onto which characters are hand-painted. These are then combined in their thousands or even millions to produce an animated film. For each movement, a separate cel is produced and the sequence of cels is then set against a production background. This process is far less laborious today as most animation is computer generated.

### COUNTERFEITS

Unlike "bootlegs", which may be packaged in a professional style but make no attempt to duplicate official releases, counterfeits are illegal copies of regular commercial records – despised by artists and the record industry, as they steal profits and royalties from the rightful owners of the music they contain. While most counterfeits reproduce million-selling albums at bargain prices, there has been a steady if small trade over the last thirty years in fake facsimiles of legendary rarities by artists such as the Beatles and Elvis Presley. In many cases, these counterfeits are so accurate that they can be extremely difficult to differentiate from the original collectibles.

### DEMOS

Demos, or "demonstration records", are those manufactured with the sole purpose of "demonstrating" a new recording. As such, they can take the form of acetates or promos, and often come under the heading of "white labels", even if they are printed with labels of another colour! Most demos are vinyl records with printed rather than handwritten labels bearing wording such as "Demonstration Record: Not For Sale". Although they are not necessarily valuable, demos by major artists – and those in specific areas, such as 1960s soul singles – can fetch high prices because they were manufactured in very limited quantities.

### FACSIMILES

A facsimile is an exact copy of an item, which may be a reproduction or a counterfeit. In the case of signatures, printed facsimiles of a star's autograph are often carried on items of memorabilia, such as guitars, toys, books, magazines or publicity photographs. These can sometimes be confused with the real thing; they also provide the raw material for unscrupulous people to create forged signatures.

## FORGERIES

In the widest sense of the term, this can apply to any fake or counterfeit version of a potential collector's item, from a record to a manuscript. In the world of pop auctions, it more often refers to autographs, handwritten artefacts or printed documents that have been faked – with varying degrees of skill – with the intention of deceiving a purchaser.

## HANDBILLS

Like "window cards", these were miniature versions of posters advertising concerts or record releases. They were usually handed out to audiences leaving a theatre at the end of a concert, and were more often than not discarded immediately. Although they are worth much less than full-size posters, handbill versions of sought-after designs can still fetch high prices at auction.

## MERCHANDISING

In the world of pop and rock collectibles, merchandising refers to mass-produced memorabilia – authorized or otherwise – that is sold to cash in on the success of a popular artist. Merchandising may take a wide variety of forms, from bubblegum cards to guitars, or badges to sets of curtains. In every case, the potential value of the item is much increased if the original packaging is intact and, ideally, unopened. Despite the large quantities in which they were made, these merchandising items were usually discarded after a few years, and this ephemeral nature can make them surprisingly valuable today.

## PIRATES

Another term for counterfeit records (see above).

## PROMOS

In the case of records, promos are any items that are manufactured for distribution to members of the media – including journalists, disc jockeys and television and radio producers – to help promote a new release. Although acetates were occasionally used for this purpose, the vast majority of promo records take one of two forms. The first, and usually most valuable, is a separate pressing from the commercial run, usually featuring different label artwork and often sleeve artwork as well to the records on sale in the shops. The second is identical to the commercial release of the record, but has a small sticker added to the cover usually bearing a message along the lines of "Promotional Record: Not For Sale".

## PROVENANCE

This is the auction-house term for the source or origins of an item that is being offered for sale. The provenance of a potential collectible can often be vital in determining its value: the better and more easily verifiable the story, the more attractive it is to the purchaser.

## PUBLICITY PICTURES

Also known as "promo pictures", "glossies" or "ten-by-eights", these black-and-white or (from the 1980s onwards) colour photographs were printed en masse and distributed to members of the media. In most cases, they only carry a nominal value, unless they have been signed by the artist (though see "Secretarial Signatures"). The use of promo pictures has been curtailed in recent years, as such images are now distributed digitally to most journalists and publications.

## REISSUES

Books are published in different editions; records are issued, and then – if the demand is there – reissued. In almost every case, a reissued record is worth much less than the original version, although the physical differences between the two can be extremely hard to distinguish. Often, however, a reissue will carry a different catalogue number, label design or date of issue from the original release, making identification easier.

## REPRODUCTIONS

Any later issue or edition of a record, poster or item of memorabilia can be classed as a reproduction. These can either be illegal or unofficial items, or "counterfeits"; or fully legal and authorized copies of a vintage collectible. In the latter case, there are usually distinguishing marks either on the item itself or its packaging to help determine whether or not it is an original. Reproductions that are ninety-nine per cent identical to the original items can often be worth a tiny fraction of their value, so it is important to be aware of this potential problem before you buy a rare artefact.

## SECRETARIAL SIGNATURES

These autographs are exact copies of the real thing, signed by members of an artist's entourage or staff to avoid the star personally having to sign hundreds or possibly thousands of photographs themselves. Usually, these well-intentioned "fakes" differ just enough from the authentic item for experts in the field to be able to differentiate them – and, in many cases, to identify the staff member who has actually signed them. Most "signed" photographs sent out by fan clubs, record companies and artists' managers during the 1950s and 1960s featured secretarial signatures. Even when fans delivered their autograph books to the dressing-room door at a theatre, it was common for staff employed by the Beatles or the Rolling Stones to sign them on the group's behalf.

## SIGNATURE MODELS

Noted guitarists, keyboardists, etc. often lend their name to particular instrument models – sometimes because they play the same models themselves, or have helped to design them, sometimes for purely commercial ends. These models usually feature a facsimile signature of the artist concerned, which can be mistaken for an original autograph by an unwary purchaser.

## SLICKS

When the artwork for a record release is ready to be printed, "slicks" are run off as a final check on the quality of the artwork, the colour, etc. They usually reproduce the sleeve artwork exactly, but are printed on large sheets of glossy white paper, which often carry the front, back and inside cover designs, together with colour guides and margins intended for use by the printer. In very special cases, when a cover design was altered at the last minute, rare and unused artwork has only survived in slick form.

## TEST PRESSINGS

Before a record or CD is distributed to the stores, a small number of copies are manufactured for the purposes of checking that the contents and sound quality are up to standard. These test pressings can usually be identified by the addition of a tiny sticker on the sleeve. In almost all cases, they carry only a small premium over the normal commercial release.

## WHITE LABELS

A generic term that covers several slightly different editions of vinyl records, created during the manufacturing process before the item goes on sale to the public. Acetates, demos, promos and test pressings are all referred to under this heading, usually because all of those discs were often pressed with plain white labels. Most often, however, the term refers to a copy of a new record, almost always a single, that is pressed for either demonstration or promotional purposes.

## WINDOW CARDS

These stiff cardboard reproductions of posters for gigs were printed in the 1950s, 1960s and 1970s, in particular, and used to advertise forthcoming events in the window of the theatre box office, local shops, etc. In the case of highly collectible posters, window cards can offer a more affordable alternative for a collector operating on a small budget.

# Christie's addresses

### AMSTERDAM

1071 JG Amsterdam
Tel: 31 (0) 20 57 55 255

### EDINBURGH

5 Wemyss Place
Edinburgh EH3 6DH
Tel: 44 (0) 131 225 4756

### GENEVA

8 Place de la Taconnerie
1204 Geneva
Tel: 41 (0) 22 319 17 66

### HONG KONG

2203-5 Alexandra House
16-20 Chater Road
Hong Kong Central
Tel: 852 2521 5396

### LONDON

8 King Street
St James's
London SW1Y 6QT
Tel: 44 (0) 20 7839 9060

### LONDON

85 Old Brompton Road
London SW7 3LD
Tel: 44 (0) 20 7581 7611

### LOS ANGELES

360 North Camden Drive
Beverly Hills CA 90210
Tel: 1 310 385 2600

### MELBOURNE

1 Darling Street
South Yarra, Melbourne
Victoria 3141
Tel: 61 (0) 3 9820 4311

### MILAN

1 Piazza Santa Maria delle Grazie
20123 Milan
Tel: 39 02 467 0141

### MONACO

Park Palace
98000 Monte Carlo
Tel: 377 97 97 11 00

### NEW YORK

20 Rockefeller Plaza
New York NY 10020
Tel: 1 212 636 2000

### ROME

Palazzo Massimo Lancellotti
Piazza Navona 114
00186 Rome
Tel: 39 06 686 3333

### SINGAPORE

Unit 3, Parklane
Goodwood Park Hotel
22 Scotts Road
Singapore 228221
Tel: 65 235 3828

### TAIPEI

13F, Suite 302, No. 207
Tun Hua South Road
Section 2
Taipei 106
Tel: 886 2 2736 3356

### TEL AVIV

4 Weizmann Street
Tel Aviv 64239
Tel: 972 (0) 3 695 0695

### ZURICH

Steinwiesplatz
8032 Zurich
Tel: 41 (0) 1 268 1010

# Bibliography

Aeppli, Felix, *The Rolling Stones 1962–1995: The Ultimate Guide*, Record Information Services, London, 1996.

Beatles, The, *The Beatles Anthology*, Cassell, London/New York, 2000.

Burgess, Paul, and Parker, Alan, *Satellite: Sex Pistols Memorabilia*, Abstract Sounds, London, 1999.

Evans, Mike, *The Art of the Beatles*, Anthony Blond, London, 1984.

Fenick, Barb, *Collecting the Beatles*, Pierian Press, Ann Arbor, 1982.

Grushkin, Paul D., *The Art of Rock*, Abbeville Press, New York, 1987.

Heylin, Clinton, *A Life in Stolen Moments: Bob Dylan Day by Day: 1941–1995*, privately published, London, 1996.

Lewisohn, Mark, *The Complete Beatles Chronicle*, Pyramid Books, London, 1992.

*Record Collector* (eds), *Rare Record Price Guide*, Parker Mead, London, various editions, 1989–2002.

Robertson, John, *The Art & Music of John Lennon*, Omnibus Press, London, 1990.

Shapiro, Harry, and Glebbeek, Caesar, *Jimi Hendrix: Electric Gypsy*, Heinemann, London, 1990.

Williams, Fred, *Rock Poster Price Guide*, Dallas Design Group, Dallas, various editions, undated.

# Index

**A**

A&M Records 39, 69
"A labels" 59
Abba 132, 139
    dolls 149, 150
acetates 58–61, 70–1, 182
album covers 167–9
*Anarchy in the UK* 135, 136
animation 169–70
Apple Records 18, 61, 118, 147, 151
art schools 164
artwork 162–73, 181
    album covers 167–9
    animation 169–70
    photographs 170–1
Aspinall, Neil 36
Atkins, Chet 82
Atlantic Recording Studios, New York 60
auction houses 14, 26, 27–8
Augsburger, Jeff 145
autographs 10, 12, 26, 29, 34–9
    concert programmes 127
    dead pop stars 38–9
    Elvis 12, 13, 36, 37–8, 126
    forgeries 36–7
    highest priced sale items 176
    secretarial signatures 36, 37, 45, 184
automobiles 102–3, 179
awards 152–61, 180

**B**

backstage passes 140–1
Baez, Joan 44, 45
Barrett, Brian 42
be-bop 86
*The Beatle Book* 132
the Beatles 8, 9, 10, 17–19, 25, 26
    album covers 167–8
    autographs 32, 39
    awards 155, 156, 160, 161
    books about 136, 138
    concert posters 110, 113
    concert programmes 28, 127, 129–30
    concert tickets 140
    costumes 90–1
    dockets from the Top Ten Club,
        Hamburg 39
    films 66, 69, 82, 118–19, 157, 169–70
    guitars 82, 83
    home-movie footage 69
    "Let it Be" 60
    letters 39–40
    merchandising 31, 144–50
    photographs 170
    and psychedelic design 114, 118
    as the Quarry Men 64, 70, 82
    recordings 57, 69
        acetates 59, 60, 61
        copyright 63
        interviews 64
        studio tapes 61
        *Yesterday and Today* "butcher cover" 28,
        66–7, 69
    replies to fan letters 39–40
    *Sgt Pepper's Lonely Hearts Club Band*
        10, 90–1, 156, 167–8
    see also Harrison, George; Lennon, John;
        McCartney, Paul; Starr, Ringo
*The Beatles Book Monthly* 132, 149
the Beatles (cartoon series) 170
Beaulieu, Priscilla 44, 100
Beck, Jeff 81
Bee Gees 158
Beefheart, Captain (Don Van Vliet) 165
Belafonte, Harry 130
Bennett, Tony 165
Berry, Chuck 54, 81
Best, Pete 39
Big Brother & the Holding Company 116,
    117
Bill Graham Presents 116
*Billy Fury Monthly* 132
Black Sabbath 118
*Blackbeat* 164
Blake, Peter 167
Blind Faith 168
Blondie 65
*Blow-Up* 121
Bolan, Marc 48–9, 70, 71, 129
Bono 12
books 126, 136–8
bootlegs 64–5, 182
Bowie, David 25
    artwork 164, 165, 172–3

award 157
concert programmes 129
*The Man Who Fell to Earth* 121
photographs 171
rare records 69
*Ziggy Stardust* costumes 90, 97
Braun, Michael 136
Brit Awards 154, 156
Britart movement 172
Britney Spears 23
Brown, Bobby 40
Brown, Ian 165
Brown, Joe 82
Buckingham, Lindsay 49
Burgess, Sonny 28
the Byrds 82
Byron, Lord 34

**C**

*Candy* (film) 120
Capitol Records 66
Cardin, Pierre 90
CarMascot Bobbin' Head dolls 148
Carr, Eric 149
cars 102–3, 179
Cash, Johnny 20
cassette tapes/recorders 55, 56
Cassidy, David 132
cels 182
Charlatans 116
Christian, Charlie 81
Christmas cards 44
Clapton, Eric 25, 62–3, 72, 164
    awards 159
    books about 138
    costumes 92
    guitars 72, 73–7, 74, 77–8, 79, 81, 82,
    83
Clark, Petula 156
the Clash, *London Calling* 168
Cline, Patsy 129
CMAs (Country Music Association Awards)
    159
Cobain, Kurt 22, 28, 74, 140
Cochran, Eddie 22, 54, 129
Cohen, Leonard 170
collectors' tips 175

"completist" collectors 27
concert posters 28, 29, 106, 109–10, 114
    highest priced sale items 179, 180
concert programmes 15, 28, 29, 34, 126–30
concert tickets 140, 141
contracts 39, 61–2, 140
Cooper, Michael, *Blinds and Shutters* 138
copyright 63, 108, 172, 173
costumes 88–99, 178
    authenticity of 91–2
counterfeits 182
Coxon, Graham 165
*Crawdaddy* magazine 135
Cream 76, 92, 113, 117
the Crickets 91, 92, 99, 129
Criss, Peter 150
Crittle, John 149

**D**
the Dakotas 60
D'Angelico, John 84
Dantalion's Chariot 111
Davie Jones & the Kingbees 69
Davies, Ray 164
Davis, Miles 86
Dean, James 130
Decca Studios 70
Deep Purple 160
demos (demonstration discs) 61, 182
Derek & the Dominos 76, 159
Dick James Music Ltd 60
Dietrich, Marlene 167
dolls
    Abba 149, 150
    Beatles 148–9
    Elvis 13
Donovan 44–5
the Doors 20, 21, 30, 48, 138, 171
    posters 109, 113
*Down Beat* (US jazz magazine) 86
drumsticks 75
Dylan, Bob 23
    album covers 168
    artwork 165
    awards 154, 156
    and backstage passes 140
    *Blonde on Blonde* 47
    books about 136, 138

*Don't Look Back* 68, 120, 121
    harmonica 27
    letters 44–5
    lyrics 47
    magazines featuring 131
    manuscripts 45–6
    photographs 170
    posters 113, 117, 120
    recordings 57, 65

**E**
the Eagles 49, 118
*Easy Rider* 121
Eck, Marty 145
*Elvis Monthly* 95, 132
EMI Records 61, 63
English, Michael 117
Eno, Brian 102
Epstein, Brian 18, 40, 42, 59, 60, 127, 144,
    146, 166
Evans, Mal 36, 46, 69

**F**
*Fabulous* magazine 124, 130, 132, 133
facsimiles 182
the Family Dog 116
*The Family Way* (film) 120–1
fan clubs 25, 33, 38
    the Beatles 40
    Rolling Stones 40, 50
fanzines 135, 136
Fawcett, Anthony 166–7
Fenick, Barb 146
film posters 108, 120–1
films 69, 155
    animated 169–70
Fleetwood Mac 46, 49, 118
Fleetwood, Mick 147
"Flying Eyeball" poster 117
the Fool 118
forgeries 36–7, 183
Franklin, Aretha 81
Free 81
Freeman, Robert 66, 170
Frehley, Ace 150
Furmanovsky, Jill 170
Fury, Billy 132

**G**
Gallagher, Noel 49
Garcia, Jerry 85, 165
Gaye, Marvin 22
Genesis publications 138
Gerry & the Pacemakers 132
Gillespie, Dizzy 86
*Girls! Girls! Girls!* (film) 97
gold discs 154, 159–61
*Goldmine* 14, 25
Goldsboro, Bobby 147
Graham, Bill 108, 114, 116
Grammy Awards 154, 155, 156
Grateful Dead 64, 85, 118, 168
    posters 109, 113, 114, 116
*The Great Rock'n'Roll Swindle* 121
Grech, Ric 49
Griffin, Rick 116, 117
Grushin, Paul, *The Art of Rock* 108
guitars 72, 74–85, 177
    Alembic 85
    Danelectro 83
    Fender Broadcaster (later Telecaster)
        78–9
    Fender Stratocasters 76–8
    Gallotone Champion 84
    Gibson ES models 79–82
    Gretsch 82
    Martin 83
    National Duolian 84
    pickguards 75
    Rickenbacker 82, 83
    signed 85
    toy 148, 149
    Zemaitis 84

**H**
Hammond, Harry 170
handbills 114, 183
Hanton, Colin 70
Hapshash & The Coloured Coat 107, 110,
*A Hard Day's Night* (film) 82, 120, 155
Harrison, George 36, 37, 60, 70
    *Concert for Bangla Desh* 92, 121
    guitars 75, 81, 82, 83
    handwritten lyrics 45–6
    *I Me Mine* (autobiography) 45–6, 138
Harry, Debbie 65

heavy metal 57
Helms, Chet 116
*Help!* (film) 66, 120, 155
Hendrix, Jimi 16, 21–2, 29, 171
    artwork 167
    autographs 12, 35, 38
    concert programmes 127
    *Electric Ladyland* 168
    guitars 74, 77
    "Hey Joe" 21
    lyrics 48
    magazines featuring 131
    opal ring 100
    posters 104, 107, 109, 112, 113, 117,
    118
    recordings 63
Herman's Hermits 147
the High Numbers (later the Who) 37
*Hit Parader* magazine 130
Hoffman, Dezo 170
Holly, Buddy 22, 26, 70
    concert programmes 127, 129
    sale of personal effects 100–1
    stage suits 91, 92
*How I Won the War* (film) 120

**I**

iconic jazz instruments 86–7
*International Times* magazine (IT) 134, 135
interviews 63–4
Ivor Novello awards 154, 159

**J**

Jackson, Michael 11, 49
    rhinestone glove 98, 99
Jagger, Mick 12, 19, 40, 50, 130
    lithograph 162
    *Performance* 121
    recordings 64–5
"James Dean syndrome" 22
Janov, Dr Arthur 46
jazz instruments 86–7
Jefferson Airplane 109, 114, 116, 168
John, Elton 85, 155
    automobile collection 102, 103
    costumes 90, 92, 93
    spectacles 90, 92
Johnson, Robert 81

Jones, Brian 19–20, 34, 38, 42, 45
    awards 155
    letter from 50–1
    snakeskin boots 88
    "teardrop" guitar 74
Joplin, Janis 22

**K**

Kelley & Mouse poster designs 116, 117
Kelley, Alton 116
King, Eric 108
The Kinks 111, 164
Kiss 16, 98, 150
*Kiss Meets the Phantom* (film) 98
Kossoff, Paul 81
Kramer, Billy J. 60
Kramer, Daniel 138

**L**

Leander, Mike 70
Led Zeppelin 108, 118
Lee, Debbie 113
Lennon, Cynthia 100, 166
Lennon, John
    artwork 164, 166–7, 172
    autographs 38
    awards 154
    and Beatles merchandising 146, 147
    books by 138
    cars 102, 118
    guitars 82–3, 84
    handwritten lyrics 46, 49
    How I Won the War 120
    interviews with 64
    *John Lennon/Plastic Ono Band* 46
    letters 40, 42, 44, 45, 98
    personal effects 98
    piano 85
    and the Quarry Men 62, 68
    recordings 60, 64, 70
    "Bad To Me" acetate 61
*Let It Be* (documentary) 120
*Let it Rock* magazine 132
letters 39–45
Lewis, Jerry Lee 20
Liebowitz, Annie 170
limited edition prints/posters/books 28
Lincoln, Abraham 101

Little Boy Blue & the Blue Boys 64
Little Richard 113
Lowe, John "Duff" 70
LSD, and the psychedelic experience 114,
    116
lyrics 44–7
    dead pop stars 46
    highest price sale items 176

**M**

McCartney, Linda 42
McCartney, Paul 84, 85, 138, 161
    artwork 164–5, 168, 169
    film music 120–1
    guitars 82, 83
    handwritten lyrics 46–7, 49
    letters 40, 42, 45
    posters 109
    and the Quarry Men 64, 70
    recordings 60, 64, 66, 70
    *Sgt Pepper* suit 91
MacGregor, Craig, *Bob Dylan: A Retrospective*
    138
McGuinn, Jim (Roger) 82
McLaren, Malcolm 39, 122
McLuhan, Marshall 116
Madonna 12, 14, 23–5, 49
    costumes 23, 90, 96, 97–8
    "Erotica 12 picture disc" 69
    posters 109
    presentation disc 152
magazines and periodicals 124, 126, 130–6
    specialist collectors 14, 23–5
    underground 134, 135
*The Magic Christian* (film) 120
*Magical Mystery Tour* (film) 69
Maharishi Mahesh Yogi 40
*The Man Who Fell to Earth* 121
Manish Boys 69
Marley, Bob 22
Marsh, Tony 113
Marshall, Jim 170
Martin, George 40, 59, 85
Martin, Janis 56
Matlock, Glen 39
Mellencamp, John 165
*Melody Maker* 42, 132
Meltzer, Richard, *The Aesthetics of Rock* 136

merchandising 28–9, 142–51, 180, 183
Mitchell, Joni 74, 165, 170
Mitchell, Mitch 77
*Modern Painters* magazine 172
Moman, Chips 81
the Monkees 10, 132, 147, 150
*Monterey Pop* 121
Monterey Pop Festival 118, 128
Moore, Scotty 81
Morrison, Jim 20, 21, 30, 138
    "Celebration of the Lizard" suite 48
    lyrics 48
    poetry collections 132–4
Moscosco, Victor 116
Mothers of Invention 117
Mouse, Stanley 116, 117
the Move 117
Murray, Rod 166
musical instruments 72–87, 179
    highest price sale items 177
    jazz 86–7
    pianos 83
    signature models 184
    see also guitars

N
Nelson, Admiral 34
*New Musical Express* 132
New Vaudeville Band 156
Newman, Ed 167
Nico 45

O
Oasis 25, 49
*Oldie-Market* 14
Ono, Yoko 80, 167
    *Grapefruit* 64
Orbison, Roy 20
Oscars 154, 155, 156, 159
Oxford Circle 109
*Oz* 134, 135

P
packaging 175
Page, Jimmy 81
Parker, Charlie "Bird" 86, 87
Parker, Colonel Tom 45, 110
Parlophone Records 40, 63

Parsons, Gram 49
*Performance* (film) 121
Perkins, Carl 20, 82
personal effects 100–1
    highest priced sale items 178
Pettifer, Doreen 40, 50
photographs 170–1
pianos 85
Pickering, Stephen, Tour 74 138
Pickett, Wilson 81
Pink Floyd 114, 168, 170
Plastic Ono Band 46
platinum discs 160
the Police 132
*Pop Hits* magazine 130
posters 104–23
    concert 28, 29, 106, 109–10, 114
    defining 106
    distinguishing original artefacts from
        reproductions 109–10
    film 108, 120–1
    psychedelic 106, 107, 109, 110, 111,
        114–18
    punk 118–20, 122–3
    signed 109
    vintage pop 110–14
Presley, Elvis 8, 10, 20–1, 26, 28, 52, 164
    and auction houses 25
    autographs 12, 13, 36, 37–8, 126
    automobile 102
    awards 154, 155, 159, 160
    books about 136
    concert programmes 125, 126
    concerts 108–10
    costumes 90, 93–7
    dolls 13
    *Elvis Monthly* 95, 132
    films 19, 81, 95, 97, 120, 126, 155
    guitars 19, 80, 81, 83
    interviews with 64
    letters 41, 42–4, 45
    magazines featuring 130, 133
    merchandising 144, 149
    personal effects 100
    pop books about 132
    posters 110–13
    rare records 69
    recordings 43, 55, 56, 57, 65, 69

stage costumes 88, 91–5
Prince 18, 25, 49, 78
progressive (prog) rock 118
"promos" (promotional records) 59, 183
promotional memorabilia 150–1
provenance 175, 183
psychedelic posters 106, 107, 109, 110, 111,
    114–18
*Psycho-Out* 121
punk rock
    fanzines 135, 136
    posters 118–20, 122–3
    recordings 55

Q
the Quarry Men 64, 70, 82
Queen 25, 151
Quicksilver Messenger Service 114, 116, 117

R
Rann, Rick 145
*Rave* magazine 130, 132
record collecting market 25, 54–8
*Record Collector* 14, 25, 70, 132
    *Rare Record Price Guide* 66
recordings 52–71
    33rpm LPs 54
    45rpm singles 54
    78rpm singles 54, 57
    acetates 58–61, 70–1, 182
    bootlegs and private recordings 64–5
    CDs 55, 58, 61, 64
    demos 61, 182
    DVDs 57
    films 69
    highest price sale items 177
    interviews 63–4
    minidiscs 57
    rare records 66–9
    reissues 183
    studio tapes 61–3
    test pressings 184
    vinyl artefacts 54–8
Redding, Otis 129
Reid, Jamie 120, 122–3, 136, 151, 168
reproductions 175, 184
rhythm & blues 12, 57
Rich, Charlie 20

Richard, Cliff 12, 109, 136
Richards, Keith 19, 40, 50, 64–5, 81
Richmond, Sophie 136
*Rolling Stone* magazine 130, 131, 135
the Rolling Stones 8–9, 19–20, 83, 121
    album covers 168
    autographs 24, 34
    awards 157
    books about 138
    concert programmes 127, 130
    guitars 83
    letters 40–2, 50–1
    lyrics 49
    merchandising 142, 144, 149–50
    posters 109, 113
    as psychedelic artists 114
    questionnaires 38, 39
    recordings 57, 59, 60–1
        bedroom tape 64–5
        "Poison Ivy" single 69
    see also Jagger, Mick; Jones, Brian;
        Richards, Keith
*The Rolling Stones Book* 132
Rory Storm & the Hurricanes 111

**S**

Scarfe, Gerald 170
Schwarz, Francie, *Body Count* 138
secretarial signatures 36, 37, 45, 184
Segal, Erich 169
the Sex Pistols 14, 65–6, 121
    album covers 168
    *Anarchy in the UK* 67, 135, 136
    autographs 39
    concert programmes 128
    contract signed outside Buckingham
        Palace 38, 39
    "God Save the Queen" 67–9, 69, 122
    *Never Mind the Bollocks* 122, 168
    posters 119, 120, 122–3
    promotional memorabilia 151
Sharp, Martin 104, 117
Sheridan, Tony 38, 40
signature models 184
Simmons, Gene 98, 150
Simon, Paul 84
*The Simpsons* 40
sitar, electric 83

"Skull & Roses" posters 117
slicks 184
Sloman, Larry, *On the Road with Bob Dylan*
    138
*Smash Hits* magazine 130
Smith, Patti
        *Horses* 168, 171
        *Kodak* 138
Smith, Pennie 168, 170
Soft Machine 117
Sonny & Cher 149, 150
Spears, Britney 25
Spice Girls 25
*Spin Out* (film) 95
Springsteen, Bruce
        awards 155
        *The E Street Shuffle* 47
        manuscripts 47
        *The River* 54
Stanley, Paul 150
Starr, Ringo 39, 61, 113, 120
        and Beatlemania merchandising 149
Status Quo 84, 85
Stewart, Ian 19, 40
Stilletoes 65
Sun Records 13, 14, 20, 28, 55, 83
Sutcliffe, Stuart 18, 83
        artwork 164, 166

**T**

T. Rex 70
Taylor, Derek, *Fifty Years Adrift* 138
Taylor, Mick 38
Teen magazine 130
*That's The Way It Is* (film) 93
tour jackets 151
tour passes 136–7
Townsend, Pete 164
toy guitars 148, 149
*The Trip* (film) 121
*Two-Lane Blacktop* 121

**U**

U2 11, 100
UFO (London underground club) 115

**V**

Valens, Ritchie 101

Van Vliet, Don (Captain Beefheart) 165
Vaughan, Ivan 64
Velvet Underground 45, 168
Vicious, Sid 22, 36, 39
Virgin Records 69

**W**

*The Wall* (animated film) 170, 171
Warhol, Andy 162, 168
Waters, Roger 170
Watts, Charlie 167
Waymouth, Nigel 117
Westwood, Vivienne 136
what's collectible 27–31
white labels 61, 184
the Who 37, 49, 85, 118
        concert programmes 127
        posters 113, 117
        recordings 62–3, 65
who's collectible 17–26
Wilde, Oscar 34
Williams, Fred, *Rock Poster Price Guide* 108
Williams, Hank 82
Williams, Paul 131, 136
Wilson, Frank 58
Wilson, Wes 107, 116
window cards 113, 184
Wonder, Stevie 10
Wood, Anita 42–4
Wood, Ronnie 38, 165
Woodstock Arts & Music Fair Festival 77,
        118, 140
*Woodstock* (film) 121
Wyman, Bill 50

**Y**

the Yardbirds 83, 113
*Yellow Submarine* (film) 120, 169–71
Young, Reggie 81
Youngbloods 109

**Z**

Zappa, Frank 132
"Zig Zag" poster 117

# Acknowledgements

PICTURE CREDITS

Page 8, David Magnus/Rex Features; 16, Stewart Cook/Rex Features; 17, Kevin Cole/Rex Features; 20, Freddie Tornberg; 22, Harry Goodwin/Rex Features; 24, RB/Redferns; 30, Dezo Hoffmann/Rex Features; 32, Harry Goodwin/Rex Features; 38, Richard Young/Rex Features; 41 (inset), Terry O'Neill/Rex Features; 47(top), Bruce Springsteen/Music Sales Ltd; 47(bottom), Eugene Adibari/Rex Features; 48, Michael Ochs Archives/Redferns; 50, Dezo Hoffmann/ Rex Features; 72, Elliott Landy/Starfile; 74, Dezo Hoffmann/Rex Features; 78, Brian Rasic/Rex Features; 99, Globe Photos Inc./Rex Features; 103, James Mann; 121 (top) Vic Fair; 123 Jamie Reid; 162, © The Andy Warhol Foundation for the Visual Arts, Inc./ARS, NY and DACS, London 2003; 164, reproduced by kind permission of Pauline Sutcliffe; 166, TDY/Rex Features; 167, Julian Hamilton/Rex Features; 168, © The Andy Warhol Foundation for the Visual Arts, Inc./ARS, NY and DACS, London 2003. Reproduced by permission of Polydor Records Ltd., UK; 171, reproduced by kind permission of Mick Rock; 173, David Bowie, *We Saw a Minotaur*, 1994, set of fourteen computer generated Iris prints with a hand coloured frontispiece, signed, dated and numbered by the artist and presented in a hand made box.

All other photographs supplied by Christie's Images

All reasonable efforts have been made to trace the relevant copyright holders of the images contained within this book. Any errors that may have occurred are inadvertent and anyone who for any reason has not been contacted is invited to write to the publishers so that a full acknowledgement can be made in future editions of this work.